About the Author

Arthur B. Evans, born in 1948 in Salem, Massachusetts, graduated *magna cum laude* with a degree in French from Tufts University in 1970, studied at the University of Paris (la Sorbonne), and received his M.A. in Humanities from Goddard College (Vermont) in 1972.

During the course of his study of Jean Cocteau, Mr. Evans has worked extensively with Dr. Frank Manchel of the University of Vermont and Dr. Robert Hammond of the State University of New York in Cortland. He has also been in contact with M. Claude Pinoteau, the technical director of Cocteau's *Le Testament d'Orphée.*

Currently living with his wife, baby daughter and dog in a small, one-room schoolhouse located in the mountains of Worcester, Vermont, Mr. Evans teaches advanced French at Montpelier (Vermont) High School.

JEAN COCTEAU
and His Films of Orphic Identity

JEAN COCTEAU
and His Films of Orphic
Identity

Arthur B. Evans

PHILADELPHIA
THE ART ALLIANCE PRESS
LONDON: ASSOCIATED UNIVERSITY PRESSES

Associated University Presses, Inc.
Cranbury, New Jersey 08512

Associated University Presses
Magdalen House
136–148 Tooley Street
London SE1 2TT, England

Library of Congress Cataloging in Publication Data

Evans, Arthur.
Jean Cocteau and his films of Orphic identity.

Bibliography: p.
Includes index.
1. Cocteau, Jean, 1889–1963. I. Title.
PN1998.A3C764   791.43′0233′0924   74-4991
ISBN 0-87982-011-X

The author wishes to thank:
Crown Publishers, Inc., for permission to quote from *Jean Cocteau* by René Gilson, translated by Ciba Vaughan, © 1969 by Crown Publishers, Inc. Used by permission of Crown Publishers, Inc.

Farrar, Strauss & Giroux, Inc. for permission to quote from *Professional Secrets: An Autobiography of Jean Cocteau* by Robert Phelps, translated by Richard Howard. Copyright © 1970 by Farrar, Strauss & Giroux, Inc. Reprinted by permission of the Author and his Agent, James Brown Associates, Inc. and with the permission of Farrar, Strauss & Giroux, Inc.

Little, Brown and Company for permission to quote from *Cocteau: A Biography* by Francis Steegmuller. Copyright © 1970 by Francis Steegmuller. Reprinted by permission of Little, Brown and Co. in association with The Atlantic Monthly Press; also by permission of Laurence Pollinger Limited, London.

The Viking Press, Inc. for permission to quote from *Three Screenplays: Orpheus, The Eternal Return, and Beauty and the Beast* by Jean Cocteau, translated by Carol Martin-Sperry. English language translation copyright © 1972 by The Viking Press. Inc. Reprinted by permission of Grossman Publishers. Also for permission to quote from *Two Screenplays: The Blood of a Poet and The Testament of Orpheus* by Jean Cocteau, translated by Carol Martin-Sperry. Translation copyright © 1968 by Grossman Publishers. Reprinted by permission of Grossman Publishers.

PRINTED IN THE UNITED STATES OF AMERICA

My warmest thanks to Dr. Seymour Simches of Tufts University for providing me with an interest in Jean Cocteau and the initial inspiration for this study; to Dr. Frank Manchel of the University of Vermont without whose patience and perseverance this study would not have been possible; to Dr. Robert Hammond of the State University of New York at Cortland for his scholarly advice and unending support; and, finally, to my wife Mary who has quietly carried the heaviest burden during the long completion of this study. Also, a special thanks to Dr. Alan Walker of Goddard College; Dr. Wade Eaton, formerly of Goddard College; and Dr. Neal Oxenhandler of Dartmouth College for their much-needed insight, criticism, and scholarship on the topic of Jean Cocteau and his poetry of the cinema.

Contents

Acknowledgments

I wish to thank the following publishers for having given me permission to quote from published works:

Dover Publications, Inc. for permission to quote from *Cocteau on the Film* by Jean Cocteau, recorded by André Fraigneau, translated by Vera Traill. Copyright (c) 1972 by Dover Publications, Inc.

Les Editions de la Table Ronde, Paris, for permission to quote from *Jean Cocteau tourne son dernier film* by Roger Pillaudin. Copyright (c) 1960 Editions de la Table Ronde. Reprinted by permission.

Elek Books Limited, London, for permission to quote from *The Hand of a Stranger (Journal d'un Inconnu)* by Jean Cocteau, translated by Alec Brown, 1956. Reprinted by permission of Elek Books Limited, London, and Editions Bernard Grasset, Paris.

E. P. Dutton & Co., Inc. for permission to quote from *Film: A Montage of Theories* by Richard Dyer MacCann. Copyright (c) 1966 by Richard Dyer MacCann. Reprinted by permission of the publishers, E. P. Dutton & Co., Inc.

Film Culture magazine for permission to quote from Ken Kelman, "Film as Poetry," Summer, 1963. Also for permission to quote from Jonas Mekas, "Hans Richter on the Nature of Film Poetry," Spring, 1957. And lastly, for permission to quote from Willard Mass, "Poetry and Film: A Symposium," Winter, 1962–63.

George Braziller, Inc. for permission to quote from *Conversations with André Gide* by Claude Mauriac, translated into English by Michel Lebeck. English translation copyright (c) 1965 by George Braziller, Inc. Reprinted with permission of the publisher and Editions Albin Michel, Paris.

Indiana University Press for permission to quote from *Filmmakers on Filmmaking: Statements on Their Art by Thirty Directors*, edited by Harry M. Geduld. Copyright (c) 1967 by Indiana University Press, Bloomington. Reprinted by permission of the publisher. Also for permission to quote from *Jean Cocteau: The History of a Poet's Age* by Wallace Fowlie. Copyright (c) 1966 by Indiana University Press, Bloomington. Reprinted by permission of the publisher.

I also thank the following for permission to reprint photographs included in this book:

Contemporary Films/McGraw-Hill for permission to reprint photographs from Jean Cocteau's *Le Testament d'Orphée.*

Raymond Rohauer for permission to reprint photographs from Jean Cocteau's *Le Sang d'un Poète.*

Robert M. Hammond and Janus Films for permission to reprint photographs from Jean Cocteau's *Orphée.*

Introduction

To what extent has the poetic film been ignored in the United States? Exactly what sort of transformation is needed to change film-narrative into film-poetry? In what way has the late French film-maker Jean Cocteau influenced this latter genre of cinema? In what way do Cocteau's three film-poems of *Le Sang d'un Poète, Orphée,* and *Le Testament d'Orphée* illustrate the current underestimation of film-poetry by the American public? How is this situation to be remedied?

The purpose of this study is to clarify and, to a certain degree, answer the above questions. Oftentimes, films that have received wide acclaim throughout Europe and the rest of the world are imported to the United States and are unexpectedly disliked by the majority of the American film-watching public. Or, much worse, such films are promptly denunciated by impatient film critics and the general public never has the chance to judge the film for themselves. Why? Is there something inherent in the films themselves that alienates American viewers, some sort of common anomaly that automatically rejects such films from the ranks of acceptable cinema? Or is there some common trait within the psychology of the American moviegoers themselves that would impede their appreciation of such films? The answers to *both* of these questions are "yes." *Film-poetry,* as it is evidenced via the "experimental" cinema of the United States as well as through many contemporary foreign films, is one such anomaly that seems to collectively disturb most American film watchers. But the blame must not rest solely upon the films. It is, to a large degree, the fault of the public itself and its complete lack of willingness to adapt its perspectives in order to accommodate the varying forms of modern cinema. The American film public, perhaps due to the extreme accessibility of the television and its almost exclusively mundane programming, has been conditioned to a static and inflexible cinematic format. Imagery, meaning, plot action, and the very structure of "good" film is defined according to rigidly set standards that have grown traditionally narrow in their scope. Foremost among these limiting criteria is the necessity for modern cinema to "entertain" by churning out a drama-filled story wherein the viewer may comfortably "lose" himself for ninety minutes or so.

In the light of such considerations, then, it seems necessary to reevaluate the role of film-poetry in contemporary cinema. The essential structure of film-poetry, how it may be attained, its cinematic and psychological objectives, and how its processes of audience interaction differ from other forms of cinema, all are important steps toward the development of a better understanding of exactly what film-poetry *is* and, as a result, how one may become better able to cope with what it offers.

With such preliminary groundwork laid, then the much-needed reevaluation of Jean Cocteau as an early film-poet may be attempted. To provide meaningful direction to such an inquiry, however, especially in the light of Cocteau's three very complex film-poems of *Le Sang d'un Poète, Orphée,* and *Le Testament d'Orphée,* an extensive "initiation" to Cocteau's highly personalized artistic vocabulary seems needed. It is hoped that, once an interpretive perspective of this type has been constructed, the succeeding analyses of Cocteau's three film-poems may prove to harbor a much deeper significance than they were originally given credit for. It is further hoped that, as an ultimate result of such a reevaluation of Jean Cocteau as one of the earliest experimenters with film-poetry, one may gain a deeper insight into the essential nature of film-poetry in general and, accordingly, be less prone to blind, uncompromising denunciation of other such films of this genre.

JEAN COCTEAU
and His Films of Orphic Identity

Note: All translations are by the author unless otherwise acknowledged.

Narrative versus Poetic Film

If cinema could be classified, it would seem that two distinct types of film have evolved from the original silent cinema: popular film (the "movies") and its more controversial cousin, the "experimental" film. Many labels and epithets have been applied to these two brands of film by many experts through the years—that is, narrative versus poetic, novel versus lyric, dramatic versus epic. But before one can speak of such matters as the actual evolution of these two progeny of silent film and then Cocteau's respective place within this development, a working definition of the two cinematic subjects seems to be in order. The differences and similarities between these two rather ambiguous classifications of film can be, perhaps, best explained through the use of the following criteria: the essential *purpose* of each type, its inherent *structure*, and the *role of the audience* to its presentation.[1]

First, consider the more popular and abundant of the two: the narrative-film. The function of this type of cinema is, obviously, narration—its primary purpose is to tell a story and, thereby, to entertain. Its dramatic, often didactic, plot follows a linear progression with respect to time. In the words of Maya Deren, the narrative breed of film is essentially "horizontal" in its movement. She, for example, makes the following distinction:

A "horizontal" development is more or less . . . a narrative development, such as occurs in drama, from action to action. . . . a "vertical" development, such as occurs in poetry, is a part plunging down, or a construction which is based on the intent of the moment.[2]

---

1. Frank Manchel, *Film Study: A Resource Guide* (Cranbury, New Jersey: Fairleigh Dickinson University Press, 1973), pp. 106–112.
2. Willard Maas, "Poetry and the Film: A Symposium," *Film Culture* 3, no. 27 (Winter 1962–3) :61.

The narrative-film has an appropriate beginning, a clearly delineated succession of events as a plot, and a climactic conclusion or denouement at the end. All the elements are usually very logically placed in time so that the spectator has no difficulty in following the flow of the story and "identifying" totally with the actors and their situations. Flashbacks and "mood" sequences are used sparingly and only when they can be directly linked to the central theme as an effective illustration of the plot. Typical examples of this form are such films as *Gone with the Wind, Love Story, Patton, Sound of Music,* and many others.

The role of the audience in the presentation of narrative-type film can perhaps be best illustrated in terms of the reason *why* people attend this brand of cinema. The large majority of audiences would most likely agree with Pauline Kael when she says:

> People go to the movies for the various ways in which movies express the experience of their lives, and as a means of avoiding and postponing the pressures they feel . . . (it) may be considered refreshment,[3]

or with Elizabeth Bowen:

> I go to the cinema for a number of different reasons. Put down roughly, they seem to fall under five headings: wish to escape, lassitude, sense of lack in my nature or my surroundings, loneliness (however passing), and natural frivolity.[4]

The craving for "entertainment," it seems, corresponds to a particular mental predisposition within the typical moviegoer. This predisposition toward relaxation, toward a deep yearning to "get away from it all," is satisfied by the essential properties of the narrative film. The film presents an impersonal story of intensified events and experiences into which the spectator can place his own identity for a short while.

It is in this sense, then, that film can be termed *entertainment*. And, further, it seems that the average movie-going public has, through the years, grown accustomed to judging *all* film according to these same standards of how well it "entertains" them. That is to

---

3. Pauline Kael, "Are Movies Going to Pieces?" in *Film: A Montage of Theories,* ed. R. MacCann (New York: E. P. Dutton and Co., 1966), p. 353.
4. Elizabeth Bowen, "Why I Go to the Cinema," in *Film: A Montage of Theories,* ed. R. D. MacCann (New York: E. P. Dutton and Co., 1966), p. 237.

say, a film is judged primarily according to how well it allows the spectator to remain relatively relaxed and anonymous, while providing for him an exciting and semicredible world of fiction into which he can project and lose himself (that is, an appealing identity substitute) .

Hence, in the narrative-type film, questions concerning meaning that are *raised* in the story are usually *answered* in the story, so that the passive anonymity and "identity displacement" of the viewer may remain accordingly intact.

Communicating meaning in film is effected through the use of sight and sound. It is through these two elements that the audience is carried into the almost trancelike state described above. The strength of the spoken word in film seems to be invested with many of the same characteristics as the written word in literature. Essentially, the spoken word needs no pictorial representation for its numerous meanings and applications to emerge successfully within the mind of the viewer. Professor Arnheim explains it this way:

> The [spoken] word refers directly to the meaning, the character, the structure of things; hence, the spiritual quality of its vision, the acuteness and succinctness of its descriptions. The writer is not tied to the physical concreteness of a given setting . . . and since he uses as his material not the actual percept but its conceptual name, he can compose his images of elements that are taken from disparate sensory sources. He does not have to worry whether the combinations are possible or even imaginable in the physical world.[5]

The strength of the visual image upon the screen as a primary conveyor of communication is, of course, unquestioned. "A picture is worth a thousand words" only approximates the communicative, hypnotic possibilities of the cinematic image. Its powers of suggestion are almost unlimited—its very nature defies the normal laws of space and time. And, in the words of V. I. Pudovkin:

> the scenariowriter must always bear in mind the fact that every sentence he writes must appear plastically upon the screen in some visible form. Consequently, it is not the words he writes that are important, but the externally expressed images that he describes in these words. . . . The lens of the camera is the eye

---

5. Rudolf Arnheim, *Film as Art* (Berkeley, California: University of California Press, 1966) , p. 206.

of the spectator. He sees and remarks only that which the director wishes to show him, or, more correctly put, that which the
director himself sees in the action concerned.[6]

However, what seems to differentiate one brand of film from another is the *interaction* of these two elements of sight and sound. The
methodology of narrative-type cinema seems oftentimes to *separate*
and *accentuate* these two aspects of film. To "entertain" the *eye*,
handsome and pleasing actors and actress are cast in title roles. It
would be, thus, unthinkable to portray the heroine of a film like
One Million Years B.C. as anything less than a Raquel Welch. Oftentimes entire scenes are cast simply to fit the stars involved, much
like the solo performance of a coloratura soprano singing an operatic
aria. Meaningful communication to the eye is also established
through such universally apparent shots as sunset scenes, dark alley-
ways, foggy decks, and speeding black sedans. The public has grown
accustomed to always seeing the "good guys" wear the white hats,
and they often feel uncomfortable if, as it was in the case of *A Clockwork Orange*, the roles are somehow reversed, or even undefined.
Meaningful dialogue, as the public expects to hear it, usually comes
in the form of, "There's something I've been meaning to say to you,
darling. . . ." or, "Sometimes a man's gotta' do what he's gotta'
do. . . ." Inevitably, the scene of spoken dialogue will show close-up
shots of the faces of the speakers, weighing their words laboriously.

It should perhaps be noted that, in the tradition of "all answers
provided" of the narrative-film, *emotional* states are "answered" by
the film as well. This function is further satisfied through the extensive use of *background music*. During the scenes of no dialogue, the
background music "tells the story"—for example action music, suspi-
cion music, apprehension music, peace music, fear music, love music.

The movie-going public has, through the years, come to adjust
its cinematic experience to this set standard of symbols—and it is
through these traditionally accepted images and dialogues that most
narrative-films communicate their respective plots. Accustomed to
this pabulum of familiar and easily recognizable film vocabulary, the
public becomes understandably perplexed and sceptical when confronted with a film that does not express itself via the same symbols.
Due to a lack of spontaneous comprehension and, accordingly, a lack

---

6. V. I. Pudovkin, "The Plastic Material," in *Film: A Montage of Theories*, ed. R. D.
MacCann (New York: E. P. Dutton and Co., 1966), pp. 24, 31.

of immediate applicability as an identity substitute, the film ceases to be "entertaining." The communicative and psychotherapeutic functions of the film are lost.

The final scenes of Kubrick's *2001: A Space Odyssey* seem to aptly clarify these two differing vocabularies of film. Essentially narrative for the most part, the plot followed a "horizontal" portrayal of the evolution of man versus his world, beginning with apes and making the rapid transition to spacemen. The plot then very logically continued with detailed excerpts of man's systematic penetration of his immediate universe. However, as the climax of the film approaches and the final dénouement is at hand, the elaborate vocabulary of the film changes drastically. The obviously chronological plot-progression stops. The entire imagery changes. The symbol-codes of meaning, established throughout the length of the film, take on a new and seemingly opaque aspect. Bursts of colors flash upon the screen, strange and transformed bedchambers are momentarily shown, a man ages an entire lifetime in a matter of seconds and, finally, the film ends with a close-up of a human embryo that seems almost to float in space. The only really familiar (though wholly indecipherable) symbol is a massive obelisk of black stone that, ironically, has been inscrutably present throughout the film.

It is evident that the interpretive vocabulary needed to translate these last few scenes of Kubrick's film into a meaningful personal application is an entirely different one than seems to suffice for the average viewer in following the plot up to that point. The images and sounds seem to be *implying* important meanings rather than trying to state them outright. Kubrick clothes his visions in a garb wholly untraditional in nature and, by so doing, removes this portion of his film from what could be called *normal narrative communication*. The audience and critical reception of this final portion of the film, as could be expected, was initially very dubious. *Newsweek* illustrates this point in saying of the film:

Kubrick spent four years and $11 million making the visionary *2001*, which was attacked by the critics for its ambiguous ending . . . but which has since been acknowltdged as one of the great feats of cinematic imagination. . . .[7]

---

7. "Kubrick's Brilliant Vision," *Newsweek*, 3 January 1972, pp. 28–29.

However, firmly justifying himself and the film's ending, Kubrick states:

> When you are implying that godlike chief entities are at work in the universe, you can't hit something like that head-on without looking like instant crackpot speculation. You've got to work through dramatic suggestion. I'm quite satisfied that *2001* had the correct ending.[8]

Now consider this second, more controversial classification of film that has evolved from the silent cinema. This particular type has been labeled as *experimental, lyric,* or *poetic,* and seems identifiable primarily as a vehicle for the portrayal of what could, perhaps, be called the artist's *interior reality.* This interior reality incorporates into its definition many diversified elements: for example, ideas, thoughts, feelings, moods, emotions, and visions. The role of film as a transmitter of these realms has never been very successfully defined. This brand of film is usually portrayed in contrast to what has been discussed as narrative-type film. Its primary purpose stems from the fact that it addresses itself to the substrata of a viewer's consciousness, rather than to his surface reasoning and "action-oriented" mentality. Some primary examples exhibiting these characteristics of film are such works as Resnais's *Last Year at Marienbad,* Buñuel's *Un Chien Andalou,* Strick's portrayal of Joyce's *Ulysses,* and, of course, the final few scenes of Kubrick's *2001.*

Depiction of "states of being," often illogical yet entirely real, seems to be the keynote for this brand of film. It is intrinsically an attempt by the filmmaker and/or director to express and communicate the abstract world of his inner, personal, lyrical visions. The film, perhaps more than any other art form, seems to be the most adaptable to this purpose. Hans Richter explains the use of cinema toward this end in saying:

> I have always been especially fascinated by the possibilities of the film to make the *invisible visible.* That relates to the abstract as it does to "fantasy" and the "inner self"—the functioning of the invisible "subconscious," which no other art can express as completely, and as drastically, as film.[9]

---

8. Ibid.
9. Jonas Mekas, "Hans Richter on the Nature of Film Poetry," *Film Culture* 3, no. 1 (Spring 1957) :6.

Carl Dreyer, the noted Danish director, summed up his feelings concerning this question of "abstraction" in an essay entitled, "Thoughts on My Craft."[10] In this essay, Dreyer recognizes the necessity for cinema to break away from the normal "reproduction of reality" and the curse of simple "photography." But he also recognizes the extreme difficulty of such an eventual evolution in film. He states:

> Human beings dislike being taken off the beaten track. They have got used by now to the correct photographic reproduction of reality, they enjoy recognizing what they already know . . . so far this capacity has been the strength of the film, but for works of art it is becoming a weakness that must be fought.[11]

Thus outlining the artistic plight of modern film, defined in terms of the public's needs and desires, Dreyer goes on to say that new creative principles must be established so that film-art may become a "pure product of the human imagination" and cease to be an "imitation of nature." One such principle, he suggests, is abstraction:

> Where is the possibility of artistic renewal in the cinema? I can only answer for myself, and I can see only one way: abstraction . . . . The artist must describe inner, not outer life. . . . Abstraction allows the director to get outside the fence with which naturalism has surrounded his medium. It allows his films to be not merely visual, but spiritual. . . . Abstraction gives him a chance of . . . replacing objective reality with his own subjective interpretation.[12]

For the purposes of this study and in the absence of a more precise term, I shall call this type of film *film-poetry,* as opposed to the previously discussed narrative-film. Of course, these facile demarcations of film are very rarely mutually exclusive. Oftentimes, as it was in the case of *2001,* one finds many instances of film-poetry within the plot of a narrative-type film. However, what characteristically divides a film into one classification or another is its *primary purpose of expression,* its raison d'être, and it is through this perspective that one must approach each film.

The essential task of the film-poem is to *externalize inner hap-*

---

10. Carl Dreyer, "Thoughts on My Craft," in *Film: A Montage of Theories,* ed. R. D. MacCann (New York: E. P. Dutton and Co., 1966) ,p. 313.
11. Ibid.
12. Ibid.

penings. The raw material of the exterior reality may or may not be used in this presentation. If not, in the manner of some contemporary "purists" who manipulate abstract geometric patterns, the visual equivalents for the internal state seem oftentimes shallow or inadequate, and even seem to exist for their plastic values alone, like graphic art-film. If, on the other hand, the elements of exterior reality are employed to create the film-poem, then these elements must undergo a transfiguration. Ken Kelman, for example, explains it this way:

> When the film-poem utilizes "real" characters and situations, it must transform them into symbols of the filmmaker's thoughts and feelings. If they retain more than a shadow of their identities, they will live too much on their own, too much as narrative, "realism," etc., and too little as sheer lyric expressions. . . . The total transformation of forms and materials into mere manifestations of the artist's state of mind is what is required. . . . The actual characters in a narrative situation take on mythical significance. They are absolutely charged with the vision of the filmmaker.[13]

A very prominent element, then, of the film-poem, in its externalization of the inner self, is that it must make manifest a "mythical significance," a symbolic language of sorts, so that the individual episodes transcend their literal sense and enter into the realm of archetype and of collective meaningfulness. Communication is, then, the most important function of the film-poem, as opposed to the entertainment function of narrative-film. Thus, the film-poem initiates a cycle that begins as subjective experience, is then transposed into an objectified presentation, and is finally "translated" back into subjective association by the viewer. An excellent example of this cycle happens in such a film as *Un Chien Andalou* of Luis Buñuel. In one scene of turbulent action where a woman seems to be discouraging the desperate attempts of a man to gain entrance to her bedroom, she slams the door on his arm. The camera then zooms in for a close-up of the hand trapped in the door and one sees hundreds of ants crawling about on the palm of this writhing hand. The author of the film desired to portray, in one very powerful image, the extreme itching hunger of this man driven mad by his craving. The simple sight of ants crawling over human flesh connotes to the viewer this rather complicated "inner reality," and the effect is much more immediate

13. Ken Kelman, "Film as Poetry," *Film Culture,* 3, no. 29 (Summer 1963) :24.

and effective than trying to accomplish the same purpose through an interchange of dialogue.

The role of the audience, then, in film-poetry differs highly from its role in narrative-film. Rather than relaxed absorption of unequivocal plot action, the spectator finds himself having ceaselessly to interact, interpret, and oftentimes ponder. Rather than entertainment, where the viewer would recognize instantly the film's vocabulary and apply it to himself, the film-poem seems almost a challenge, and to respond to the challenge the viewer must decode the artist's visionary presentation and *adapt* its multiple meanings to his own self. Thus, the question is not, "What did the artist mean by. . . ?", but rather, "What happens to *me* and what do *I* see when. . . ?"

To further complicate matters for the average viewer, the creative process of the film-poem is highly different from that of narrative-film. Whereas the narrative-film, or any commercial film, must follow an ironclad script from beginning to end (to properly convey the meaning of the plot in clear-cut terms), the film-poem "grows" in the actual shooting. The director "feels" his way through the shots and sequences, and the finished product may or may not resemble the conscious blueprint constructed for it at the beginning. In the words of director Richter:

> There is a kind of script, there is a general direction, there is an aim, a meaning, a mood in the process of production. But all that grows is not foreseen. It is a result of the creative process itself. It is not so much planning as it is feeling along the path which the theme takes. In other words, the material you accumulate during the shooting is more or less raw material; though it has been planned to contribute to a specific scene, plan, or aim, it might, in the end, assume a different meaning altogether. This I would call "sensitive improvisation." This listening to oneself as well as to the material which you accumulate is essential to a film-poem. . . .
>
> One has to count upon spontaneous inspiration, urges, the often quoted "subconscious." In having the ear open to them, the conscious plans, made in advance, might suddenly—and will often —hamper the work one really has in mind. . . .[14]

Thus, one can truly pity the plight of the "uninitiated" viewer who, trying his utmost to "understand," wishes to discover the symbols

---

14. Mekas, p. 7.

and secrets of "what the author meant"—that is, demanding of his conscious mind a deciphering of the language of his unconscious.

Communication of these inner realities through the film-poem is established through the imaginative *marriage* of the elements of sight and sound. The image is of particular importance, for it is through the imagery that the film-poem tries to visually construct and communicate its essentials. If the art of the film, in general terms, consists of starting with individual shots and building first into scenes and then sequences, then the "film-poet" applies a different set of criteria from the "film-narrator" in constructing his imagery. Shots are often taken for their *singular, individual* beauty or symbolism and, when added to a series of other such shots, the sequence that develops may suggest a strange but meaningful continuity, oftentimes previously unforeseen (*see* note 14 above). What is important to the poetic film construct, then, is its communicative and evocative powers through *visual suggestion.*

The tools of manipulating imagery—montage, superimposition, and the like—become, thus, paramount to the filmmaker's intentions, for they rule the manner in which the film is going to "talk" to and interact with its audience. An example of this visual communication is listed by Kelman in the following excerpt from his essay concerning film-poetry:

> An early, rudimentary, and very famous example of internal impressionism, and a constructed (not free) association, occurs in Pudovkin's *Mother.* Here the young imprisoned revolutionary receives a note informing him of plans for imminent escape. His emotions on reading this are conveyed to us by a close-up of his smiling mouth, and then a rapid succession of shots blending into each other: a laughing child, water sparkling in the sun, and so forth, all meant to render the prisoner's surge of joy. The attempt here is to find direct visual equivalents for an internal state; thereby to suggest exactly the same feeling to the spectator. The fact that the images are detached entirely from the situation, and even the character—but rather, represent universally valid associations of joy, applied to a specific circumstance—makes this a fair sample of fragmentary film-poem.[15]

Further, the film of all possible art forms, bears the closest affini-

---

15. Kelman, p. 22.

ties to the unconscious and the state of dream. Outlining these similarities, Anais Nin states:

> It is impressionistic, it takes place on several levels at once, it is composed of montages, intrusions from the past, composite pictures and memories. The camera more exactly than words is capable of reflecting our inner life and revealing the metamorphosis which takes place between a realistic scene and the way our moods color, distort, alter, or heighten that scene as through a prism.[16]

And Arthur Miller, participating in a symposium dedicated to the discussion of poetry and film, contributed a further dimension to this idea of film and dreams when he observed:

> I think that the film is the closest mechanical aesthetic device that man has ever made to the structure of a dream. In a dream, montage is of the essence, as a superimposition of images in a dream is quite ordinary. The cutting is from symbolic point to symbolic point. No time wasted.[17]

And the meaning or significance of a particular dream, its very power as it unleashes itself against the eye of the consciousness, comes directly from its suggestive imagery. It seems perfectly appropriate, therefore, that the film-poem, having as its raison d'être the externalization of the inner life, should coordinate its manner of presentation to what Susanne Langer calls the *dream mode*.

> Drama is "like" action in its being causal, creating a total imminent experience, a personal "future" or destiny. Cinema is "like" dream in the mode of its presentation; it creates a virtual present, an order of direct apparition. That is the mode of dream.[18]

Drawing its technique from intrinsic similarities to its subject matter, the film-poem's images are timeless. That is to say, the viewer of a film-poem is plunged into the incorporeal dimension of "virtual present" and loses his worldly sense of linear direction. Then, through a sense of spontaneous and intuitive discovery, the viewer may see, portrayed in a montage of suggestive images, strangely significant

16. Anais Nin, "Poetics of the Film," *Film Culture* 31 (Winter 1963–64) :14.
17. Maas, p. 58.
18. Susanne Langer, *Feeling and Form* (New York: Charles Scribner's Sons, 1953) . p. 412.

counterparts to what he feels inside. Communication has then been effected, at least in part, and the ultimate purpose of the film-poem has been achieved.

The communicative power of the word (spoken or written) versus the image has been a topic of much debate through the ages. There have been these who have praised the development of the "talkie" as an important breakthrough in art. There have been those who considered the intrusion of spoken dialogue into film a disaster.

It seems, however, that within the film-world of today a "leveling" effect is taking place. Commercial narrative-type films seem to be becoming more "poetic" in their cinematic methodology (particularly in terms of image constructs and elements of montage). Similarly, "experimental" films seem to be incorporating into their structure more dialogue and a greater continuity of design. Thus, the polarization that has affected the film industry since the early years of cinema seems now to be entering a period of compromise and coalescence. The effect of this current attitude change upon the "word versus image" controversy has been foreseeable—*balance* is now the key. Both modes of the communication of meaning must operate together within the film to transmit fully the totality of the cinematic experience to the spectator. The innate power of this balanced coordination of word and image, each supplementing the other's strength, can be seen in the works of such contemporary filmmakers as Bergman, Fellini, Antonioni, Resnais, Truffaut, Kubrick, and a host of others.

It is through this framework of contrasting narrative-film and poetic-film that one must approach the cinematographic works of Jean Cocteau. As seems to be becoming increasingly clear to many literary and film scholars, Cocteau stands as a forefather to many "contemporary" developments in cinematic art. W. Maas, during a symposium on poetry and film, made the following observation:

Now, Ezra Pound said in a definition of the image that it is an emotional and intellectual complex caught in an instant of time. It's a very direct and quick way of saying things, a lyric way of saying things, while the way a dramatist says things is by putting the characters that speak back and forth into conflict. We know that you can't have any sort of situation, poetic or otherwise, without dramatic conflict. I agree with that, but it's quite different in developing a narrative action than presenting it imagistically and quickly, and I think in film you can do that. You can do it by word; you can do it by visual image, and by the combination of the two, which is a very complicated thing. Though mentioned, no one here tonight has talked very extensively about Jean Cocteau's *Blood of a Poet*. Anybody that sees that, sees the perfect welding of the two. It can be done. Though he is the father of the poetic film, Jean Cocteau does not have many forebears.[19]

Cocteau, since the early 1930s, has been using cinematic themes and techniques usually associated only with the modern poetry of today. A partisan of no literary or cinematic "school," Cocteau was a stubborn independent who learned the science of film on his own —trial and error. A playwright and poet, Cocteau applied his literary talents to the screen, and many of his films are directly identifiable, in terms of technique, to his poetic works. The balance between his use of word and image on the screen is unmistakable. Recognizing Cocteau as a forebear to many of the contemporary tendencies in film, Robert Richardson, in his study *Literature and Film,* states the following opinion with regard to this balance:

> It was also Cocteau who referred to his films as studies of "the frontier incidents between one world and another." The frontier he meant is that between the real and the apparent, between the actual world and the camera's world, between dreams and art, and between death and life. His descriptions may be given another meaning, whether he intended it or not, for his films and those of a number of other gifted men are "frontier incidents" also in the sense that they take place between the world of words and the world of images.[20]

However, what seems to be of primary importance to this study was the incessant rejection of Cocteau's poetic films during the time when they were first presented. Particularly within the United States, where Americans seem to rely heavily upon what the "authorities" say about any given work of art (especially foreign art) before they can establish for themselves its essential value, Cocteau's films of poetry have (until recently) generally received a most unjustified condemnation.

Throughout the last decade, however, many fine studies have been done on Cocteau as a *literary* figure, and the various scholars

19. Maas, p. 62.
20. Robert Richardson, *Literature and Film* (Bloomington, Indiana: Indiana University Press, 1969), p. 16.

of these words have, from time to time, extended their research into Cocteau's films. Thanks to such literary critics as Neal Oxenhandler, Robert Hammond, Roger Lannes, André Fraigneau, Wallace Fowlie, Margaret Crosland, Jean-Jacques Kihm, Elizabeth Sprigge, Frederick Brown, Francis Steegmuller, and a host of others, the path toward acceptable film criticism of Cocteau seems now well paved. Through such individuals the public is now offered a multitude of interpretations, analyses, clarifications, and comments on such film-poems as *Le Sang d'un Poète, Orphée,* and, though to a lesser degree, *Le Testament d'Orphée.*

Each of these aforementioned scholars chooses a *perspective* and, within its confines, constructs his respective "interpretation" of what the film-poem is suggesting and communicating. This perspective may be developed from the study of some fundamental characteristics of Cocteau's *themes* (his homosexuality, need to be admired, and so forth) or from some fundamental elements of Cocteau's *poetic ideas* ("Zones," "angel," "invisibility," and so forth) or, finally, from the point of view of Cocteau's *public* (how others saw him, reacted to him, and so on).

Each successive perspective of interpretation should be considered as equally valid. All recognize the necessity for "initiation" into Cocteau's personal visionary world in order to explain the many artistic outgrowths of this sphere. All have established common points of reference through which the film-poem may communicate to the viewer. These many attempts toward the construction of a framework of meaning for Cocteau's works aid intuitively in the comprehension of his film-poetry, although they do not and can never successfully *explain* the film-poems. But, then again, most were never originally meant to.

The author himself, when asked for a definitive statement concerning the correct meaning of his film *Le Sang d'un Poète,* replied after some thought:

> I search for only the relief and the detail of the images that came forth from the great night of the human body. I then immediately adopted them as the documentary scenes of another realm. That is why this film which possesses a single style . . . presents a multiple surface to exegesis. Its exegeses were innumerable. When asked about any one of them, I would always find it difficult to answer. . . .[21]

---

21. Jean Cocteau, *Two Screenplays: The Blood of a Poet, The Testament Of Orpheus,* trans. Carol Martin-Sperry (Baltimore, Maryland: Penguin Books, 1968), pp. 3–4.

The initial purpose of the remainder of this study is twofold. The vastly differing vocabulary of film-poetry as compared to film-narrative necessitates a lengthy investigation into the personal nomenclature of Cocteau as a poet. To what is the author alluding when he uses such seemingly significant symbols as angels, Zones, and mirrors? What are the specific characteristics of this "Marvelous" of which he speaks so often? What are the bonds linking Cocteau's visions, his "fantasized" works, and his self-proclaimed "discipline" of technique? And what interpretive stance is his audience expected to assume when "experiencing" a film such as *Le Sang d'un Poète, Orphée,* or *Le Testament d'Orphée?*

The answers to these and other such pertinent questions should facilitate the comprehension of Cocteau's fundamental vocabulary in his film-poetry. Having thus established a common point of reference, this study will seek further to construct and clarify one particular theme crucial to the consideration of the three films in question: the theme of "Orphic identity." Cocteau's affinity to the mythic, and especially to the Orpheus myth, was of a special importance to him and his identity as a poet. It is this preoccupation that seems to determine Cocteau's "communicative" purposes in *Le Sang d'un Poète, Orphée* and *Le Testament d'Orphée.* The origins of this strange and heretofore overlooked fixation by Cocteau, its characteristics, its influences, and its significance will be respectively investigated.

Having thus established a frame of reference through which the work of Cocteau may be approached, the final step of this study will be to construct a thematic interpretation of the three autobiographical films previously mentioned.

It is hoped that, as an ultimate result of this study, a heretofore "extrapolative" realm of Jean Cocteau's life and works will be rendered a bit more lucid and less prone to blind, unfounded denunciation.

Thematic Guideposts
for a Comprehension
of Cocteau

A. Introduction

To become truly "initiated" to the poetic visions of Jean Cocteau, one must first assume a perspective shared by the author himself. This perspective, once taken, should then clarify Cocteau's motives for doing what he did and the manner in which he did it. Although a detailed study of Cocteau's life would be helpful to the construction of such a perspective, the purposes of this particular study can not feasibly include such an extensive biography.[1] Through a comprehensive investigation of his professed poetic philosophy and his ensuing identity as a poet, however, one can become sufficiently familiar with Cocteau's hermetic terminology, and perhaps begin to "understand" the majority of his recurring themes, whether they be in his novels, poetry, theater, or films.

Perhaps the most logical method to follow in effecting this familiarity is one which an author himself is faced with in creating an actual work of art. This creative progression begins, for Cocteau, with the inner poetic vision—the *inspiration*. The next step involves the *portrayal* of this vision—an effective representation using, as a vehicle toward this end, some appropriate art form. To evaluate the efficiency of the attempted poetic communication, the final step (and,

---

1. For an excellent and complete life history of Cocteau, Francis Steegmuller's study entitled, *Cocteau: A Biography* (Boston: Little, Brown and Co.. 1970), is admirably well suited to the purposes as described above. Another very good study is Elizabeth Sprigge and Jean-Jacques Kihm's *Jean Cocteau: The Man and the Mirror* (New York: Coward-McCann, Inc., 1968).

for Cocteau, perhaps the most important) concerns the receptivity and *appreciation* of the public to the work of art presented. It is through this three-step progression that the poet defines himself and his art. It would seem not unreasonable, therefore, that to follow this path of investigation would ultimately "initiate" the prospective viewer of Cocteau's film-poems to his operative vocabulary and, in so doing, render these films infinitely more meaningful.

B. Realization

What is poetry? Where does it come from? What is a poet? Does the poet create poetry or does poetry create the poet? The answers to such questions are crucial to a deeper comprehension of Jean Cocteau. Yet, such answers are not readily obvious. The term *poet* seems a bit confining when considering the master *bricoleur* Cocteau, who has to his credit some fifty volumes of poems, plays, novels, memoirs, diaries, and criticism, not to mention his drawings, films, murals, stage sets, ballets, tapestries, sculptures, and music. Encyclopedias are always a little perplexed as how to classify him, since there is hardly any art form or genre that he did not, at one time or another, utilize.

Yet Cocteau, throughout his life, insisted that the only epithet that could define him accurately would be the term *poet*. And, further, his many varied works of art were all successive manifestations of what he conceived as *poetry*. In the largest possible sense, therefore, to be a poet was, for Cocteau, to be a *creator of art*; and poetry stood as the ensuing *artistic creation, regardless of genre or form*. It was through this perspective that Cocteau defined his "poetry of the novel," his "poetry of the theater," and, later, his "poetry of the cinema."

But the concept of poetry itself, outside of the framework of literary and artistic terminology, had a much deeper and more profound meaning for Jean Cocteau. Poetry is the stepping-stone toward a contact, a communication with another world. To form a bridge between the reality of routine, everyday life, and the reality of the "beyond" seems to be the primary purpose of Cocteau's conception of poetry. Whether the poetry takes the form of novel, verse, images, or sound is relatively unimportant. In speaking of this characteristic of art forms, Cocteau has stated in his essay entitled "Le Secret Professionnel":

> I state that . . . music, painting, sculpture, architecture, dance,
> verse, dramatics, and this muse which I term as Cinema, the
> Tenth Muse, are the snares with which man tries to capture po-
> etry for our usage.[2]

Although the distinguishing attributes of the actual vehicle are of less
consequence to Cocteau, how well it "captures poetry for our usage,"
how well it provides the link between these two spheres of reality
seems to be of major import.[3] Poetry, then, seems to be definable for
Cocteau as a communicative "state of being"—a mental and spiritual
"way of seeing"—which, once effected through an art form, can permit man to rise above the everyday barriers of space and time and
penetrate the "beyond." Cocteau summarizes this purpose of poetry
saying: "Poetry simulates a reality of which our world possesses only
an intuition."[4]

The position of the poet seems directly definable within Cocteau's
framework of poetry. The poet is the inspired mouthpiece, the messenger for the beyond, whose responsibility it is to convey, somehow,
the spirit of poetry, and in so doing, to help to facilitate the ultimate
communication between the viewer and this other world. The poet
thus stands as an oracle—the coded enigmas that pass through his
mouth are only in a small measure his own. In true Romantic tradition, the role of the poet is that of being "possessed," of uttering
truths that originate deep within himself but which are not his. The
poet, thus, belongs to his poetry and not the poetry to the poet. Cocteau, again in "Le Secret Professionnel," elaborates upon this theme
and states: "The poet's role is a humble one—he is at the orders of
his night."[5] Cocteau's "night," in this case, can perhaps be qualified as
a sort of Jungian unconsciousness through which the poet receives
his visions. In his *Journal d'un Inconnu*, Cocteau clarifies this rather
nebulous term, and underscores the role of the poet as a simple messenger, a middleman, between the beyond and the eventual artistic
manifestation.

> It is true that any poet is the recipient of orders. But these come
> from a tenebrosity which centuries have piled up in him, and of

---

2. Jean Cocteau, "Le Secret Professionnel," in *Le Rappel à l'Ordre* (Paris: Editions Stock, 1926), p. 189.
3. Cf. section C of this chapter, "Portrayal."
4. Jean Cocteau, *The Hand of a Stranger (Journal d'un Inconnu)*, trans. Alec Brown (London: Elek Books, 1956), p. 172.
5. Cocteau, "Le Secret Professionnel," p. 186.

which he is but the humble vehicle, tenebrosity into which. . . .
he cannot go.[6]

The position of the poet, then, seems to be almost one of schizo-
phrenia. He walks the boundary separating one world from another,
experiencing both, yet residing permanently in neither. Further, it
seems the poet's responsibility to try, as a "medium," to form a means
of indirect contact between these two worlds—the vehicle for this
contact being the poetry experienced through his "imitative" artistic
creations. And it is interesting to note that, according to Cocteau,
the poet never tastes the fruits of his labors—his role is simply to
convey. Reminiscent of the preceding definition of the film-poem,
where each viewer sees his own poetry, the poet's job is to convey
what is within him and not to try to interpret its multiple meanings.
Cocteau's play *Les Chevaliers de la Table Ronde* seems to point this
out in Act III when Galahad presents the Holy Grail to King Arthur
and his court:

ARTHUR.   Galahad, why do you ask us to explain the Grail? Gala-
          had, is it not you who should be explaining it to us?
GALAHAD. I cannot see it.
ARTHUR.   You!
GALAHAD. I shall never see it. I am the one who makes it visible
          to others.[7]

Recognizing this characteristic go-between pose of the poet, Cocteau became especially attracted to the poetic image of the *angel*.
Having once made reference to the metaphor that life and death are
but opposite sides of the same coin, Cocteau conceives of the shuttling back and forth between these two states of being as the prerogative of both poets and angels. It is through this phoenixlike cyclical
movement that the poet comes to know truth. Like the angel,
he plays the role of the messenger of another realm and seeks only
to communicate its secrets to a normally cynical and questioning
host of "unbelievers." The angel soon developed into one of Cocteau's
favorite "personalized" myths. During the turbulent years following
the death of his beloved friend Radiguet, when he grew more and
more preoccupied with opium, death, mirrors, and other various

---

6. Cocteau, *The Hand of a Stranger*, p. 5.
7. Jean Cocteau, *Professional Secrets: An Autobiography of Jean Cocteau*, ed. Robert
   Phelps, trans. Richard Howard (New York: Farrar, Straus, and Giroux, 1970),
   pp. 263–64.

items that would subsequently be incorporated into his works, Cocteau first made mention of his theories concerning angels. In his *Le Rappel à l'Ordre* (completed in 1926) he writes:

> Always according to this luxury of using, without commentary, certain terms usually interpreted by readers in an altogether different manner than by us, poets speak often of angels.[8]

The author then goes on to paint a rather shocking portrait of what he considers to be the primary characteristics of these celestial beings. Divorcing the concept of angels from any tangible religious ideology, and defining them not in terms of God or heaven but simply in terms of the "beyond," Cocteau stresses their ability to "pass from the visible to the invisible with the powerful splash of a high-diver." The angel, the author states, is found between the human and the inhuman and the "radiating movement which composes him prevents his being seen." Further, this special breed of angel "suffocates the living and tears their soul from them without being at all touched." Finally, Cocteau completes his discussion of the angel with an interesting but rather tangential extrapolation concerning the "fall of angels" and the "fall of angles" (the two terms supposedly being synonymous in Hebrew).

Throughout Cocteau's extensive essay concerning his personally embossed definition of angels, however, there seems an undercurrent of implied meaning. To what extent is the author speaking in autobiographical terms? To what extent does this rather unconventional description of angels correlate with the professed role of the poet? What Cocteau seems to be describing, under the metaphorical guise of angels, are the characteristics of what he had previously called the poet's "night"—that is, the undeniable and oftentimes cruel presence of the "beyond," living within the poet and using him as a vehicle for its own manifestation. This angelic presence comes and goes, passes from the "visible to the invisible" and, when engaged in the act of inspiring the poet, must truly seem to be "suffocating the living and tearing their soul from them." Thus, Cocteau seems to equate the poet's *inspiration* directly with the inhabitation of the poet by an angel.

The strength of this observation is enhanced by the fact that most poets are obsessed or haunted by a unique state of mind that

---

8. Cocteau, "Le Secret Professionnel," p. 201.

he terms *angelism*. And it is primarily due to this state that the poet can be considered truly authentic. Outlining the observable effects of this angelism of poets, Cocteau states:

> Indifference, egoism, tender pity, cruelty, suffering from contacts, purity in debauchery, mixture of violent tastes for the pleasures of the earth and scorn for them, naive amorality . . . these are the signs for that which we call "angelism" and which all true poets possess whether he writes, paints, sculpts, or sings. Few people admit it, for few feel real poetry. . . .[9]

The tone of his discussion seems obviously autobiographical, and the question comes to mind whether Cocteau, as the innocent oracle of his inner "angel," is indirectly weaving a fabric toward some type of eventual self-exoneration for his conduct or life-style. Whatever the case, the concept of angelism for Cocteau seems to be essentially an eruption of the divine in the human, and stands as a clarifying factor in the investigation of the relationship of poet to poetry.[10]

To further clarify the poet's "realization" of his poetry, Cocteau has made extensive references to the metaphor of "death," through his works, personal interviews, and autobiographical essays. Using the term figuratively, Cocteau seems to designate as *death* the actual transit made by poets and angels between the exterior everyday reality and the realms of the "beyond." But since, as the preceding discussion illustrates, every true poet carries within himself his own angel that is the source of his inspiration, Cocteau's reference to death seems to signify the poet's "leaving of this world" to join the presence of this interior companion.

Initially, this metaphor seems perfectly apropos for Cocteau's purposes, since, normally, one must pass through the physical state of death before meeting the heavenly hosts. Thus, by using this term with regard to the poet's inspiration, Cocteau insures a clear public comprehension of his terminology. This metaphor of death seems additionally well chosen when correlated to Cocteau's view that the inspired poet is but an oracle—that is, the poet's exterior consciousness "dies" as he communicates with his inner angel. And, last, Cocteau seems to portray in this term the physical and mental suffering that a poet must endure during this profound poetic experience. With

---

9. Cocteau, "Le Secret Professionnel," p. 205.
10. Several interesting studies have been made concerning the relationship of angels to men. Foremost among them (although no mention of Cocteau is made within its pages) is Theodora Ward's *Men and Angels* (New York: Viking Press, 1969).

these aspects of his definition in mind, Cocteau accordingly equates "inspiration" with "expiration":

> Valery confessed that for him the poem was a matter of artistry, not inspiration. But the problem is more serious, for inspiration is merely expiration; things do not come from the outside, but from the inside. . . .[11]

To effect this "death journey" into himself, to expire in order to be inspired, Cocteau oftentimes relied heavily upon the "transporting" medium of opium. Cocteau's literary adversaries have often criticized him concerning his use of opium, saying that the true poet needs no such crutch to become inspired. To these arguments, he points out that it is not the drug that causes the inspiration—the poet as "chosen prophet" has no say whatever in that matter. As one of the selected few inhabited by an angel, the poet is an inspired individual whether he be willing or not. Opium, however, acts as a catalyst to aid the poet in coming to grips and communicating with his inner guest. Inspiration is by no means the cause-effect resultant, nor even aided itself, by the use of opium. It is the *man* who finds opium helpful in bringing about this mandatory "death" of the exterior and enabling him to experience more fully what is within him. Indeed, everyone has an unknown realm of reality inside him, if he but knew how to make contact effectively with it. Cocteau generalizes this need saying:

> Each of us carries something compressed inside himself, like those Japanese flowers which unfold when immersed in water. Opium plays the part of water.[12]

And, with reference to the use of opium by poets, as a vehicle with which to aid in the poet's "death," the author draws the analogy: "Life and death are as far apart from one another as heads and tails of a coin, but opium goes through the coin."[13]

In any event, it could be reasonably argued that Cocteau's entire poetic philosophy, his life-style, and his very approach to his art were radically and permanently altered during his years of opium addiction from 1924 to 1929. It was during this time, and that immediately

---

11. Cocteau, *Professional Secrets*, p. 278.
12. Ibid., p. 130.
13. Ibid., p. 178.

following, that the author came to find his personalized mythology of mirrors, angels, truthful lies, invisibility, and, inevitably, his preoccupation with the literal and figurative aspects of death. A deeper investigation into this portion of Cocteau's life and his association with opium, thus, seems definitely warranted and, indeed, almost mandatory if one is to construct a meaningful perspective through which to view the author and his works.

The story begins with a young man named Raymond Radiguet. Born in 1903, the eldest son of a commercial Parisian artist, Radiguet, by the age of fifteen, had become known among the poets and artists of Paris as a "poet prodigy," and grew to be a close friend of such celebrities as Max Jacob, André Salmon, Juan Gris, and Igor Stravinsky. Via Max Jacob, in 1918, Cocteau came to make the acquaintance of this precocious youngster (Cocteau was fourteen years his senior) and their friendship developed rapidly. They worked on their poetry together, traveled together, and Cocteau soon came to describe Radiguet as his "adopted son." Among the more notable works to come out of this intimate friendship was Cocteau's essay "Le Secret Professionnel" (1921–22), the theatrical productions of *Les Mariés de la Tour Eiffel* (1924), and *Antigone* (1922–23), a collection of poetry entitled *Plain-Chant* (1923), and two novels *Le Grand Ecart* (1922–23) and *Thomas l'Imposteur* (1923). To Radiguet's credit, two novels were to develop: *Le Diable au Corps* (1921–22) and *Le Bal du Comte d'Orgel* (1922–23). It was during this feverish period of literary creativity that Radiguet countered Diaghilev's old command to Cocteau of "astonish me" with the observation that "elegance consists in *not* astonishing." (This comment was to have a lasting effect upon Cocteau's subsequent artistic methodology.)

Rising rapidly in public renown, and equally in notoriety, Radiguet and Cocteau's friendship was not long to continue, however. The former, now a celebrity in his own right, went from party to party and began to do a great deal of drinking. In addition to his customary two bottles per day of whiskey and gin, Radiguet also began to smoke opium on a regular basis. His debts began to soar as he constantly moved from hotel to hotel. He gradually withdrew himself from Cocteau's company, refusing to be called "Madame Cocteau" by jesting friends.

On 12 December 1923, Raymond Radiguet died alone in a Parisian hospital, having contracted typhoid. His death dealt an immeasurable blow to Cocteau. Recovering from a state of shock immediately following his notification of his friend's death, Cocteau expressed his grief in a letter to Abbé Mugnier:

> The death of my poor boy has been the finishing blow for me. . . .
> Death would be better than this half-death . . . I suffer night and
> day . . . I shall never write again. . . .[14]

It was not long after that Cocteau began to smoke opium in heavy and repeated doses.

The following five years produced remarkable changes in the then thirty-five-year-old author. Alternately undergoing the physical cravings of addiction and the pangs of withdrawal in a local sanatorium, Cocteau spent his time in morbid meditation of death and quasi-religious self-questionings. His health waned and he became more of a recluse than he had ever been. His creativity as an artist and writer did not seem to suffer, however, and actually seemed to thrive on his new-found life-style (particularly in the quiet and undisturbed seclusion of the sanatorium). Cocteau came to identify his effervescent creativity of this period directly with his use of opium, and subsequently seemed to consider that his repeated addiction to this drug was not of his own doing—his work, his "angel," demanded this course of action of its powerless host. In his diary of *Opium: Journal of Intoxication,* where he elaborately describes his incessant attraction to and repulsion by the drug, Cocteau points out:

> Cured, I feel empty, poor, sick at heart. . . . The work which exploits me needs opium . . . once again I am its dupe . . . I shall smoke again if my work wants me to.[15]

It was especially during this period of drug usage and cure that the author's creative life seemed to develop into a specific cyclical pattern. He would smoke heavily for a number of months, and then during his voluntary seclusion at the sanatorium for supposed purposes of disintoxication, he would feverishly transpose his acquired visions into drawings, poetry, plays, and other various artistic configurations. In a preface to one of his collections of rather Surrealistic-looking drawings of this time, Cocteau states:

> Trying hard not to write, I drew. Otherwise my hand would grow frantic from four o'clock to midnight. In this way I kept myself

---

14. Jean Cocteau, taken from Francis Steegmuller's *Cocteau: A Biography* (Boston: Little, Brown, and Company, 1970), p. 316.
15. Cocteau, *Professional Secrets,* p. 132.

occupied and at the same time provided a young intern with data on my symptoms.[16]

These drawings show a marked preoccupation with eyes, hands, and various corpselike postures of death. Cocteau's fixation upon the mirror, which was later to become one of his favorite "mythified" poetic symbols, seems to have had its origin during this period. Living in Villefranche and smoking steadily, Cocteau spent days sitting in front of a mirror, drawing his own rather distended portrait; "watching himself die," he later asserts.

It was also during this period that the author, perhaps feeling some opium-induced nostalgia for his childhood religion, began to have long conversations with Jacques Maritain concerning religious theology, opium, and the role of the poet in life and death (still with Radiguet in mind no doubt). The image of the crucifixion and subsequent rebirth of Christ particularly drew the attention of Cocteau, who saw in this phoenixlike metaphor a reflection of his own moral, physical, and spiritual predicament as an artist and as a man. It would not be unreasonable to state that at its origin, Cocteau's entire theory concerning the nature of "angels" (as previously discussed) was also the direct result of this strange juxtaposition of opium and religious doctrine.

In any event, the death of Radiguet and the ensuing period of opium did much to transform Cocteau from the lighthearted and frivolous young poet of the Parisian salons to the infinitely more serious and introverted poet of his later years. It was during this portion of his turbulent life that Cocteau "found himself"—at least in the measure where it relates to his identity as a poet. The metaphor of "death" became for him an integral stepping-stone toward the comprehension of his life and his theories of poetry. It is from this vantage-point of death and rebirth, therefore, that one can begin to see the "Orphic" nature of Cocteau in his more autobiographical works—a perspective of interpretation to be constructed later in this study.

Thus, the question of inspiration and the poet's muse for Jean Cocteau seems definable primarily through the metaphors of "death" and "angelism." Through the former the poet arrives at a communication with the latter, and the groundwork for the viewer's bridge to and contact with the "beyond" is laid. As always, the poet is merely

---

16. Cocteau, Steegmuller's *Cocteau*, p. 340.

the "humble servant," at the orders of his "night," and serves mankind as the intermediary for the enigmatic manifestations of poetry as dictated by his "angel."

But the poet, as a "medium," has one final duty to perform in trying to convey his visions. He must somehow fashion a just and effective representation of his visions, utilizing the normally inadequate raw material of the outside world. It is only after successful completion of this final duty that the poet will have established a true contact between his viewers and the "beyond." This is the poet's challenge: to remain credible to his audience, and yet to remain true to the essential character of his visions.

C. Portrayal

Having discussed Jean Cocteau's philosophic position concerning the definitions of poet and poetry, and his beliefs regarding the complex nature of the poet's inspiration-expiration, the question remains as to *how* the transference takes place between the interior vision and the exterior manifestation of that vision. In what way does the artist go about representing his inner "messages" via some chosen art form? Cocteau, as a poet, was much concerned with this problematic necessity and considered this aspect of the poet's identity as the most demanding. In a brief but very concise axiom characterizing this quandary he states: "Find first. Search after."[17]

If any single term can adequately pinpoint Cocteau's operative strategy in portraying his visions, it must be his irrefutable sense of *discipline*. If his ideas and poetic convictions are essentially avant-garde by classification, then his methods must be termed almost classical by design, especially in comparison with the Dada and Surrealist movements of his era. From his first text of artistic criticism, *Le Coq et l'Arlequin*, Cocteau affirms:

A poet always has too many words in his vocabulary, a painter too many colors on his palette, a musician too many notes on his clavier.[18]

---

17. Cocteau, *The Hand of a Stranger*, p. 169.
18. Jean Cocteau, *Le Coq et l'Arlequin*, taken from text of Jean-Jacques Kihm's *Cocteau* (Paris: Editions Gallimard, 1960), p. 253.

The final creation of a work of art, for Cocteau, demands of the poet a severe self-discipline and, above all, a refined sense of *choice*. True art can not exist without a great amount of selective editing, revisions, corrections, and adaptations. The skill of "artistry" seems, therefore, an inherent aspect of Cocteau's artistic aesthetic. It is in this manner that the poet seems to emerge as a self-determining figure, someone who consciously makes decisive and heavily pondered decisions regarding the evolution of his craft. In this measure, the poet is self-willed and self-critical, delineating his chosen paths and following them unhesitatingly.

But is not this entire doctrine of self-determination and artistic selectivity a bit foreign to the consideration of Jean Cocteau, particularly in the light of the preceding discussions of "unwilling oracles," "inner angels," and figurative "deaths?" Not at all, for the bond that links these two facets of the creative process is, for Cocteau, one of cause and effect. The poet may have no choice in the matter of his initial inspiration and his destiny as a "carrier"; nevertheless, because he wishes to render the subsequent representation of his visions as true to life as he possibly can, he is forced to become extremely meticulous and discretionary concerning his methods of presentation. Thus, it is only through the utilization of the strictest rigor and control that the artist can faithfully depict and communicate the fruits of his inspiration. Though the subject matter may be fantastic by nature, and would perhaps accommodate itself better to portrayal through a sort of nebulous fairy tale, Cocteau repeatedly emphasizes the necessity for precision and realism. In speaking of Cocteau's *Beauty and the Beast*, René Gilson makes the following observation of the author's methodology:

> All of the aesthetic—as well as the ethic—of these "fairy tales without fairies" is contained in this definition: flee the fairies, the mists, the spectacular and suavely falsified, the fantastic, the poetic, and the irreality of convention in order to better attain Poetry through order, rigor, the invention of new elements, beauty of simple lines, the harmony of perfect rhythms.[19]

And while praising Bérard, the technical director of his film *Orphée,* Cocteau is quick to point out:

> He was the only one to understand that the marvelous cannot be

---

19. René Gilson, *Jean Cocteau,* Cinéma d'Aujourd'hui Series, no. 27, trans. Ciba Vaughan (New York: Crown Publishers, 1964), p. 56.

evoked through vagueness, and that mystery exists only in precise things. He also knew that nothing is easier to create than false fantasy in the film world.[20]

To illustrate his feelings concerning the poet's need for rigorous discipline in the practice of his profession, Cocteau has often made reference to the metaphor of the acrobat. From the canvasses of Picasso, the poetry of Max Jacob and Apollinaire, and a daredevil transvestite of the high wire called *Barbette,* Cocteau inherited this important and very expressive image. Perched high above the circus's sawdust floor, precariously balanced upon a very thin wire, the acrobat's life depends upon his perfected equilibrium. His art is one of sensitivity and courage and it demands constant, unfailing concentration. Simulating the borderline stance of the poet between the real world and the "beyond," the acrobat is always one footfall away from a permanent residence in the latter. Further, like the poet, when not engaged in his perilous and skilled art, he becomes once again a "normal" human, indistinguishable in a crowd of people. Cocteau perhaps saw in this image, as well, a partial incarnation of his ideas concerning angels—half-way between this world and the next, inspiring those who take heed, and forcing those who would visually communicate with them to "raise their eyes toward the heavens" (in a literal as well as figurative sense). Whatever the case, Cocteau's unique fascination with the high-wire acrobats was to subsist for his entire life and he often used them in his autobiographical essays as a clarification of the poet's mandatory discipline in his work.

Cocteau's disciplined techniques and forms lead him, rather ironically, to the realm of what he liked to term the *Marvelous.* Essentially, this epithet seems to designate the composite characteristics of what could be called the *atmosphere* of Cocteau's works. And it is within this cloak of the Marvelous that Cocteau defines what he feels to be true poetry. According to one scholar, Cocteau's Marvelous can be clarified in the following terms:

> The Marvelous—that which the cinema especially, thanks to its techniques, succeeds in imposing upon even the most rebellious— proceeds from the "chasm which opens in a most inexplicable manner": coincidence, chance, and "fortunate" encounters between the inattention of the author and the faculty of enchantment of the spectator.[21]

20. Jean Cocteau, taken from the text of André Fraigneau's *Cocteau par Lui-même* (Paris: Editions de Seuil, 1957), p. 104.
21. Gerard Mourgue, *Jean Cocteau* (Paris: Edition Universitaires, 1965), p. 74.

And the author himself, in his book *La Difficulté d'Etre,* explains the term thus:

> The Marvelous would be, then (since a prodigy wouldn't know how to be a prodigy except in the measure of when a natural phenomenon still escapes us) not a miracle, disheartening by its resulting disorder, but a simple human miracle, very common-place, which consists of giving to persons and objects a certain "unusualness" which defies analysis.[22]

This sense of intangible yet ever-present mystery superimposed onto very commonplace people and events seems the heart of Cocteau's "unusualness which defies analysis." The Marvelous would seem to proceed from finding wonder in the usually unnoticed and taken-for-granted components of everyday reality. When speaking of the elements of this "simple human miracle" in a taped interview with André Fraigneau, Cocteau drew the analogy of a child's wondrous fascination over the fact that sugar melts in water and yet, in the bathtub, he does not. It is this special childlike perspective of constant discovery and awe that seems to typify the author's definition of the Marvelous and the resulting atmosphere of his works. But one very necessary prerequisite of this manner of perception is the capacity of the viewer to *believe.* And it is the poet's job to assure the credibility of his work so that the viewer may unhesitatingly believe —thus, the ever-present need for strict discipline of technique in the poet's presentation.

One major tool that Cocteau repeatedly and successfully uses to construct his world of the Marvelous is the mechanism of *myth.* One finds in his works a considerable usage of two general types of mythologies. First of all, he reworks and adapts to his purposes the standard, ancient, and universal myths of Greece, Rome, and the Middle Ages. In this category could be classified such works as *Antigone, Oedipe-Roi, Bacchus, La Machine Infernale* (the Sphinx), *La Belle et la Bête, Les Chevaliers de la Table Ronde, L'Eternel Retour* (a modernization of the myth of Tristan and Iseult), and, of course, *Orphée.* Second, and oftentimes within the actual fabric of the above, Cocteau extensively utilizes what he terms his own "personal mythology." These myths are apparent only to those who have become sufficiently "initiated" to Cocteau's life and art. They are intimate to the author and meaningless when considered apart from him. One could incorporate into this personalized code of *symbols* (although Cocteau

---

22. Jean Cocteau, *La Difficulté d'Etre* (Monaco: Edition du Rocher, 1957), p. 78.

would shudder at the use of the term) his unique fixation upon mirrors, "where Death comes and goes. . . ," his angel Heurtebise, Dargelos "le coq" of the schoolboys, the five-pointed star, masks, statues, horses, blood, motorcycles, and a host of other items inherent to his artistic vocabulary.

The reasons for Cocteau's use of myth (of the former type) as an active tool in portraying the Marvelous are twofold. First, myth had a very powerful psychological attraction for Cocteau in terms of his own personal identity as a poet; it is this portion of himself and his art that shall be treated later at length under "Orphic identity." But also, and what pertains specifically to the question of his techniques of portrayal, Cocteau saw in the use of myth a vehicle admirably well suited to his needs for the construction of "believability"—a vital step in the poetic communicative process and the audience perception of the Marvelous. The very definition and function of myth itself would seem to underscore its inherent value for Cocteau. According to some dictionaries, myth may be defined along the following lines: "an account of legendary times and heroic, magical tales, or a story, the origin of which is forgotten, in the form of a fantasized allegory that helps explain a natural occurrence, a historical fact, or a philosophic idea."[23] That is to say, a myth is a *surnatural* or *unreal* story, that materialized into a concrete reality for the minds of those ancients who wished to explain the inexplicable, communicate the incommunicable. For the ancients, a myth was worth nothing if one was not able to *believe* in it—once believed, it offered a humanistic and revealing glimpse into the unfathomable workings of the beyond and its relationship to human life. In this manner, myth served as not only a "scientific" instrument of explanation, but also as a method of fulfilling a quasi-religious social necessity as well. Seen in this light, Cocteau's choice of mythical prototypes as the framework for his poetic endeavors seems quite apropos, particularly when comparing their function to the author's essential objectives in and through his works.

Another significant tool that Cocteau uses to portray his world of the Marvelous is the art form of the *film*. Considering the cinema as an unparalleled instrument in the communication of poetry, Cocteau accordingly dubbed it "Cinema, the Tenth Muse," and subsequently

---

23. Taken from *Webster's New Collegiate Dictionary*, 2nd ed. (Springfield, Massachusetts: G. and C. Merriam Co., 1956) , p. 558; and the *Petit Larousse* (Paris: Librarie Larousse, 1967) , p. 686.

came to use it as his most preferred poetic vehicle. However, to ennoble and renovate this "Tenth Muse," to the end that she may better utilize her innate capabilities, Cocteau first had to react against the then current public conceptions of "cinema": that is, "movies," designating a superficial and shallow distraction or amusement, forgotten as soon as seen. Expressing his reaction against this "earthly" form of cinema, Cocteau invented the term "cinematograph"—designating a film created by a poet, whose sole raison d'être is to be a vehicle for his thought and never a "commodity bowing to the laws of consumerism." He explained:

> What is commonly called *cinema* has not been, up till now, a pretext for thought. People walk in, look (a little), listen (a little), walk out, and forget. Whereas the cinematograph, as I understand it, is a powerful weapon for the projection of thought, even into a crowd unwilling to accept it.[24]

> The cinematograph is an art. It will deliver itself from the slavery of industry of which the platitudes do not incriminate it more than do bad canvasses and bad books discredit the arts of painting and literature.[25]

But the master poet-painter-dramatist, Cocteau, was only a neophyte to this trade that required special skills and technical know-how then unknown to him (c. 1930). And he seemed to realize this fact well, saying: "Before film art can be worthy of a writer, the writer must become worthy of film art."[26]

Nevertheless, without hesitation and with many hopes, Cocteau plunged himself into his new-found genre—the immediate result being *Le Sang d'un Poète,* a film of "poetry" created in complete liberty and with a naiveté just as complete. All the same, with his ceaseless audacity, his sureness, and his strict demands for style, Cocteau was determined to push back what he called the "dead rules of cinema." His initial cinematographic goals were thus twofold: he must first learn the complex methodology of the art and, at the same time, change its "rules" so that it might better conform to the author's usage of a vehicle for the Marvelous. It was these two obstacles that

24. André Fraigneau, *Cocteau on the Film,* trans. Vera Traill (New York: Dover Publications, Inc., 1972) , p. 14.
25. Jean Cocteau, *The Difficulty of Being,* trans. Elizabeth Sprigge (London: Peter Owens Publishers, 1966) , p. 49.
26. Fraigneau, *Cocteau on the Film,* p. 21.

Cocteau felt that he had to overcome in the making of *Le Sang d'un Poète*. He explained:

> I've been completely free only with *Le Sang d'un Poéte* because it was privately commissioned (by the Vicomte de Noailles, just as Buñuel's *L'Age d'Or*), and because I did not know anything about film art. I invented it for myself as I went along, and used it like a draughtsman dipping his finger for the first time in Indian ink and smudging a sheet of paper with it. Originally Charles de Noailles commissioned me to make an animated cartoon, but I soon realized that a cartoon would require a technique and a team nonexistent at that time in France. Therefore, I suggested making a film as free as a cartoon, by choosing faces and locations that would correspond to the freedom of a designer who invents his own works.[27]

Thus, with the desire to "move this great machine of dreams, to grapple with the angel of light . . . the angels of space and time," Cocteau completed his first piece of "poetry of the cinema." In contrast to the major technical difficulties that he admittedly confronted during his short apprenticeship to the art of the cinema (money considerations, censorship, and so on), Cocteau nevertheless found in the art form of the cinematograph an exciting implement to further his artistic visions. Elaborating upon the possibilities of the cinematograph, he states:

> Time and Space. Film art is the only art form that allows us to dominate both. . . . We are free to manipulate as we please a world in which nothing seems to permit man to overcome his limitations.[28]

And it is perhaps due to this sense of freedom, this capability of tampering with those very elements of sight and sound, space and time, that dominate the viewer's perception of life's experiences, that Cocteau saw in his cinematograph not only a perfect poetic vehicle for his hermetic visions, but also an unrivaled instrument for the creation of believability for his audiences. Whatever the case, Cocteau was to use the genre of film again and again throughout the rest of his life as his most preferred communicative device. And it would be through film that he would ultimately attempt to express his innermost identity as a poet, completing a cycle begun in *Le Sang d'un*

27. Ibid., pp. 16–17.
28. Ibid., p. 115.

Poète, continuing in *Orphée,* and terminating with his cinematographic epitaph of *Le Testament d'Orphée.*

In using the cinematograph as a powerful tool toward the construction of the Marvelous, Cocteau was, by necessity, much concerned with questions of cinematic technique. Indeed, what seems to triumph in these film-poems was the *manner* in which he created them, gave them life, and intensely animated an otherwise concrete and scientific audio-visual phenomenon. The manner in which Cocteau gives life to his "visual poems" is accentuated by "streams of images" that separate themselves one from the other by their own proper "discontinuity." In the same way that he disperses the element of *time* (the tumbling of the factory chimney in *Le Sang d'un Poète,* for example), Cocteau abolished the laws of space through his magical and enchanting imagery. When asked by André Fraigneau for a clarification of his philosophy concerning the manipulation of imagery in his films, Cocteau replied:

> The cinematograph requires a syntax. This syntax is obtained through the connection and clash between images. No wonder that the peculiarity of such a syntax (our style) expressed in visual terms seems disconcerting to spectators accustomed to slapdash translations and to the articles in their morning paper.[29]

The technique of "connection and clash" of images seems to epitomize Cocteau's uniqueness as an early film director. In his *La Difficulté d'Etre,* the author again alludes to this brand of cinematic imagery saying: "The persons of these films obey the rules of elves—as soon as one perceives them, they disappear."[30] The perceptive film critic Parker Tyler, in his book *The Magic and Myth of the Movies,* offers a clarification of Cocteau's "connection and clash" theories concerning film imagery. According to Mr. Tyler,

> each instant on the screen presents to us the mythic prototypes of our own consciousness or, perhaps, our unconscious. The "evocative" power of the cinema is, in this manner, greater than any other art form.[31]

It is this "evocative" quality of the cinematic image that lies at the heart of film-art's potency as a communicative device. Accordingly,

---

29. Ibid., p. 15.
30. Cocteau, *The Difficulty of Being,* p. 50.
31. Parker Tyler, *The Magic and Myth of the Movies* (New York: Citadel Press, 1965), p. 17.

the true strength of the image comes not simply from its appeal to and interaction with the clear and reasonable thinking mind but, on the contrary, it is judged by how well it can penetrate the subconscious, private world of hidden dreams and intuitions within each viewer. This, then, would seem to define the true communicative power of the cinematic imagery of Jean Cocteau.

In this light, therefore, it is not surprising to note that Cocteau seems vastly more interested in making his images "discontinuous" rather that "continuous." In effect, he wishes each individual series of images to live and evoke to the fullest extent of their individual capabilities and not simply "fill in the gaps" between the action-dialogues of the ongoing plot. In this manner, Cocteau allows the film to communicate with the viewer on a much deeper level of consciousness and meaning than the conventional narrative-type film, and, in so doing, removes his film for the realm of mere "entertainment." The author explains:

> My primary concern in a film is to prevent the images from flowing, oppose them to each other, to anchor them and join them without destroying their relief. But it is precisely that deplorable flow that is called "cinema" by critics, who mistake it for style. It is commonly said that such and such a film is perhaps good, but that it is "not cinema," or that it lacks beauty but is "cinema," and so on. This is forcing the cinematograph to be mere entertainment instead of a vehicle for thought. And this is what leads our judges to condemn in two hours and fifty lines a film epitomizing twenty years of work and experience.[32]

It is interesting to note that Cocteau's insistent desire to define his cinematograph as a "vehicle for thought"—in contrast to its presupposed role as "entertainment"—seems to correlate very strongly with the definitions of "film-poetry" versus "film-narrative" discussed at the beginning of this study.

In any event, a deeper comprehension of what Cocteau called his "poetry of the cinema" seems directly linked to an understanding of his technical use of various cinematic elements such as imagery. It is through his manipulation of "discontinuous" images that the author projects upon a visual screen his interior visions—these visions of personal and collective dreams, this strange "illogical logic" at all times present within each individual psyche. And it seems precisely this cinematic technique, these "qualitative progressions" of

32. Fraigneau, *Cocteau on the Film*, pp. 15–16.

images, that helps to construct the elusive dimension of the Marvelous and house the true poetry of Cocteau's "Tenth Muse."

Cocteau's previously discussed fixation upon the metaphor of "death" when speaking of his personally embossed definitions of a poet and poetry seems, once again, to be one of his favorite terms when speaking of the technical portrayal of his visions. For Cocteau, there seem to be five successive figurative deaths involved in the transference of his poetry from within himself to the outside world. These five deaths could be listed as follows: the death of the poet's "opium consciousness," the death of traditional art forms, the death of the poet during actual creation, the death of the purity of the original vision, and last, the death of the poet's presence with his finished work of art. Each death, for Cocteau, is mandatory for the eventual manifestation of the desired work of art.

The first of such deaths occurs when the poet, having received his "orders" or inspiration, must renounce this "otherworld consciousness" and return to the harsh realities of everyday life. It is from the raw material of this exterior reality that he is obliged to fashion a just representation of his vision. But, before he can proceed with his task, he must first "return to life"—and his active intercourse with the "beyond" must momentarily die. For a long period in Cocteau's life this death was particularly distressing, due to the fact that he had used opium to facilitate his initial contact with the "other consciousness," and to return to a normal state of mind required a certain amount of physical suffering through withdrawal. Cocteau describes the death of his "opium consciousness" and the cruel reawakening of his worldly self as follows:

> For a long time sleep was my refuge. The prospect of waking kept me from sleeping well and dictated my dreams. In the morning I no longer had the courage to unfold my life. Reality and dream were superimposed: a bedraggled smear. I would get up, shave, dress, and let whoever was in my room take me . . . anywhere. Oh those mornings! When you are thrown into dirty water, you must swim. . . .[33]

Having thus become resurrected from the "beyond," the poet then ironically becomes himself an agent of death. In order to create an efficient and worthy representation of his visions, the poet must bring about the "death" of the old, traditional art forms—and, through

---

33. Cocteau, *Professional Secrets*, p. 110.

bold and imaginative experimentation, he must somehow replace these archaic genres and "rules" with artistic forms more appropriate to his needs. Cocteau was always a firm advocate of audacious yet disciplined experimentation toward the discovery of new pathways of poetic expression, and he incorporates this feeling into his definition of what it is to be a poet:

> The public does not like the rules to be changed. But what is a poet? He's a man who changes the rules.[34]

One can not help but feel that Cocteau's many technical "gimmicks," particularly noticeable in such films as *Orphée, La Belle et la Bête,* and *Le Testament d'Orphée,* are a direct outgrowth of this need for new methods of portrayal, to communicate the incommunicable. Such gimmicks as Cocteau's use of a vat of mercury to film Death's passage through a mirror in *Orphée,* for example, stand as hallmarks of modern cinematic innovation and imagination.

The third figurative death in the process of the portrayal of poetry occurs during the actual labor of creation. During this period when the artist is actively engaged in shooting scenes, applying colors to canvas, or scratching words upon paper, he removes all else from his mind and, in terms of his recognizance of the world around him, he dies. He may not literally "work himself to death," but his work, effectively, becomes his life and he ignores all else to the extent that he may become physically ill. René Gilson observes:

> Jean Cocteau, then, was not a passive admirer of the ingenious work from which he profited. He, from personal necessity, continually paid with his person. He was not a dabbler who clambered over all the ladders, catwalks, and props, searing his eyes beneath the spotlights. He had to live in the set, to sense himself how one might live it, in order to bring his characters to life in it afterward. . . . But with what profound joy did he himself perform his task of cinematic creation, even when forced, as during the filming of *Beauty and the Beast,* to overcome dreadful pain and to push his physical and emotional endurance to impossible limits. During the filming of his last movie, *Testament of Orpheus,* Francois-Regis Bastide . . . was horrified to see Cocteau burn up hours when he should have been asleep, and [Bastide] cried: "Such mad imprudence! He's endangering himself!"[35]

---

34. G. M. Bovay, *Cinéma; Un Oeil Ouvert sur le Monde* (Lausanne, Switz.: Editions Clairfontaine, 1952), p. 16.
35. Gilson, 18–19.

For all of his perseverance, imagination, and toil, however, the poet can not avoid realizing a fourth death in his work. This is the inevitable death of the purity of his original vision as compared to the author's rendition of it via the concrete representation. By definition, the portrayal of any event or experience is not the event or experience itself, and must suffer a lack of immediate actuality, at least for the poet. To portray is to only bring back partially to life the complex wholeness of the original vision. And, according to Cocteau, the issue is further complicated by the fact that the representation itself seems oftentimes to fight against and impede its own eventual self-manifestation. Battling the forces of bad weather, technical breakdowns, and temperamental stage props, Cocteau, during the filming of *Le Testament d'Orphée,* grew quite frustrated with the progress being made and, while pointing an accusing finger at one such prop, exclaimed:

> It's he! It's he who doesn't want it! He has become a living personage! And he resists us! You'll see! He's going to give us trouble all night. . . ! It's the wickedness of objects. You make them and then they turn aaginst you. You must be crazy to want to create a work of art. There are none in Nature. Nature detests them and resists them.[36]

Ultimately overcoming such technical difficulties, however, the poet completes his work; but what results from his efforts is usually much different from what he had originally intended. The crux of the problem seems to derive from the fact that to reproduce accurately his visions via an art form requires an unavoidable *adaptation* to that art form in terms of practicality, workability, and finance. Thus, due to either technical necessity or financial feasibility (particularly within the film industry), the poet must do his best with what he has. Further, the finalized work of art differs from the original inspiration to the measure that it "grows" during the actual filming. As previously discussed, the evolution of a film-poem is a creative process in itself and prone to much "sensitive improvisation": for example, during the filming of *Le Testament d'Orphée* where Minerva strikes down the poet with her lance, a supersonic jet passed over the site and Cocteau, joyous, decided to include the resulting sonic boom as an integral part of the scene. In any event, a certain transfiguration takes

---

36. Roger Pillaudin, *Jean Cocteau Tourne Son Dernier Film* (Paris: La Table Ronde, 1960), p. 53.

place between the author's conception of his inspiration and the form that this inspiration will eventually take as a concrete work of art in the outside world. It is due to this variation, perhaps not entirely unwanted, that the essential purity of the original vision is lost or, as some might say, improved upon. However one may see it, it constitutes one of the figurative deaths in the process of portrayal for Cocteau.

The final figurative death for the poet has to do neither with his inspiration nor with the actual transposing of it into art. It results, for Cocteau, from the innate antipathy of a creator coexisting with his creation. For the work to truly "live" on its own and subsequently become immortal, unencumbered by the weight of the author's social identity and/or "legend," the poet must die. Cocteau put it this way:

> We are dead men vis-à-vis a work which we have written, since after the words "The End," the "I" who wrote the work is dead. The work is posthumous.[37]

> The poet is dead. Long live the poet.[38]

This final death signifies for the poet the completion of his task of portrayal. As a result of this death, the poetry *is* the poet—the poet, having materialized that which was sacred within him, becomes empty. His identity has been assumed by his work of art—it lives its and his life and carries its and his name, while he humbly awaits the next call of his inner "angel," when his identity can once more be reborn through inspiration.

It is, then, through a series of figurative deaths that the poet achieves a portrayal of his visions. And it is not without a great amount of discipline, perhaps of "knowing how to die," that he is able to portray effectively his world of the Marvelous and subsequently communicate his poetry. In the use of cinema and myth Cocteau found admirable tools for this task; for, above all, it seemed mandatory for the audience to become able to believe in the normally unbelievable in order to perceive true poetry.

But one final step remains, and one that Cocteau deemed to be the most important of all. It is as a direct result of this step that the poet ascertains whether or not his attempt at poetic communication,

37. Bovay, p. 16.
38. Cocteau, *Professional Secrets*, p. 314.

his artistic bridge between the prospective viewer and the beyond, has been successful. This step involves the work of art's *reception* by the public and their reaction to what it offers. In addition, pertaining specifically to a deeper and more comprehensive understanding of Cocteau, the *poet's* reaction to the audience-reception of his works should offer some illuminating insight into his highly complex relationship of poet, poetry, and public. It is through an investigation of this final step in the creative process that Cocteau's thematic vocabulary can be rendered a bit more meaningful and his artistic motivations made a bit less obscure.

D. Reception

Now turn to the final step of the poet's creative process, his reception in the outside world. As with the two previous aspects of Cocteau's art, this relationship between the poet, his poetry, and his public stands as a predominant factor in determining the author's somewhat complex symbolic vocabulary. And, given the fact that a true "initiation" to the author's hermetic nomenclature would necessitate investigation into all three realms of his trade, this particular phase of his artistic endeavor seems to merit close scrutiny.

It would not be unreasonable to say that one of the largest factors influencing Jean Cocteau's life as a poet and also as a man was his tumultuous relationship to his public. This quarrelsome kinship, for Cocteau, was a curious mixture of unceasing love for his admirers and plaintive scorn for his critics. There is perhaps no other contemporary author who has achieved so much notoriety during his lifetime and, at the same time, watched his works remain relatively unread. As Wallace Fowlie observes:

> Of all the really famous writers admitted to the ranks of the French Academy, Cocteau holds the distinction of probably being the least well known. His name is famous throughout the world, but his works are not familiar.[39]

This fact exerted a tremendous amount of influence upon Cocteau's eventual artistic vocabulary and his very identity as a poet as expressed through *Le Sang d'un Poète*, *Orphée*, and *Le Testament*

---

39. Jean Cocteau, *The Journals of Jean Cocteau*, ed. and trans. Wallace Fowlie (Bloomington, Indiana: Indiana University Press, 1964), pp. 3–4.

d'Orphée. Both as a poet and as a man, it often seems true that, as
Frederick Brown once put it, "He was fated to crave love in order to
be."[40] But, more than a simple "craving for love," Cocteau desired
most to close the credibility gap between himself and his public; he
wanted to be *understood and believed.* It is in reference to this particular sensitivity of Cocteau's that Margaret Crosland aptly states:

> He did not so much want "rave" reviews for his work but
> he wanted understanding. Most of all a poet wants to be believed.
> He did not want to be either a magician or an acrobat—that was
> too easy. He wanted people to stand back from the picture and
> look at him properly.[41]

However, for Cocteau, the task was not so easily accomplished.
Due to the hermetic nature of his vocabulary and the corresponding
need for "initiation" to his poetic expression of the Marvelous, Cocteau's works were not immediately popular with the movie-going
public of his time. And, seemingly obsessed with the idea that his
identity as a poet is in large part defined by the audience-reception
of his works, Cocteau came to see himself as the misunderstood and
persecuted hero of poetry. It is not incidental that, during his religious affiliations with Jacques Maritain, Cocteau grew to believe that
the Christian image of Christ on the cross seemed an appropriate
symbol designating the lonely agony of the poet.[42]

What Cocteau felt that his public lacked, in order truly to comprehend the nature of his works, was a certain measure of childlike
naiveté, a predisposition toward "letting themselves go." To make
the "unreal real" demands not only, for the poet, a strict discipline
of technique and form, but also it demands of the audience a certain
willingness to believe in the normally unbelievable. To fully "experience" a work of art, according to Cocteau, one must be able to
identify totally with the characters and actions on the screen. This
transformation involves a complete loss of self-consciousness and an
equally complete absorption in the work presented. It is only
through this "collective hypnosis," as discussed at the beginning of
this study, that the author's communicative purposes can be achieved.

---

40. Frederick Brown, *An Impersonation of Angels* (New York: Viking Press, 1968), p. 55.
41. Margaret Crosland, *Jean Cocteau, A Biography* (London: Peter Nevill Editions, 1955), p. 128.
42. Later, his poem entitled "La Crucifixion" (written in 1945–46) elaborated this particular theme.

When, during an interview, Cocteau was asked about this audience characteristic, he replied:

> I am a very good audience. When I am in the theatre I succeed in "abstracting" myself completely. . . . It is very difficult for the public to abstract itself and identify with a work when its toes are walked over, it is made to stand up and look over others' heads, it has electric lights flashed in its face, and it is being sold icecream cones . . . a film-showing is a ceremonial. If the ceremony is lost, all is lost.[43]

Thus, if the "atmosphere of ceremony" is lost and the audience is unresponsive and/or unsuited to collective hypnosis, the communication initiated by the poet through the work of art remains incomplete. This state of affairs angers the unknowing audience, who feel themselves somehow "cheated" of their due entertainment, and, consequently, they collectively blame the artist responsible for their deception. Cocteau, the accused, defends himself saying:

> The public does not expect what the true poet gives. The public is disappointed—it feels he has not kept his promises.[44]

And: "The public believes that, if the language is not poetic, it is not a film of poetry. . . ."[45] But the damage has been done and no after-the-fact excuses can remedy the situation or soothe the ruffled tempers of an angered public. The artist, by trying to introduce innovative techniques and imaginative imagery toward a conscientious portrayal of his visions, has succeeded only in arousing scepticism, alienation, and hostility. By trying to communicate effectively outside of the established framework of the previously discussed traditional symbol-codes and standards, accepted modes of meaning, the artist is considered a fake—if, indeed, an artist at all. And, if the artist persists in his foolhardy attempts to deceive and confuse, his ensuing notoriety quickly becomes widespread.

A master at converting public defeats into personal victories, Cocteau adapted his social and artistic notoriety into his ever-flowering poetic philosophy. Seemingly proud of his noble efforts despite the public's oftentimes contrary opinions, Cocteau developed his theory

---

43. Bovay, p. 15.
44. Cocteau, *Professional Secrets*, p. 87.
45. Bovay, p. 15.

of the poet's and his creations' essential "invisibility," that is, that which is unseen. He explains:

> I am unquestionably the most obscure and the most celebrated of poets. Sometimes this makes me sad, for fame terrifies me and I like to excite only affection. . . . But as soon as I think upon it I scorn my melancholy, telling myself that my visibility, a product of idiotic legends, does protect my invisibility, wrapping it round with a thick glittering coat of armour which can withstand any blows with impunity. When they think to wound me, they wound a stranger whom I prefer not to know. . . .[46]

The complex relationship between the artist, his creations, and his public is, thus, one of apparent paradox. The artist is seen, yet unseen. The dichotomy seems to revolve around the fact that there is an essential duality to the poet's identity and that of his poetry when considered in a social context. With regard to both, the public views only the picturesque outer shell and fails to comprehend the meaningful inner workings of each. That is to say, the central essence of both artist and creation remains invisible to the spectator who is much more concerned with the readily apparent, the visible. In terms of Cocteau, the man, this public fixation upon only the visible reduces him to a simple incarnation of his "legend" and cancels out the possibility of his being taken seriously via his creations. And, accordingly, his works remain visible only as extensions of his legend, thereby adding more fuel to the flames of his notoriety. Their true intent, composition, and significance—their individual identity independent of their creator—remain invisible to public awareness.[47]

Finding these metaphors of visibility and invisibility rather fascinating and quite well suited to his needs, Cocteau extrapolated further and further in his writings the applicability of these two themes. Rather than remaining an apparent excuse for his esoteric style in the face of public criticism, it became for him something much more substantial to the question of the general role of a poet and the nature of his craft. First, in terms of his techniques of portrayal, Coc-

---

46. Cocteau, *The Hand of a Stranger*, p. 7..
47. One excellent case in point is provided by Bosley Crowther in his review of *Le Testament d'Orphée*. His entire discussion of this film seems irrevocably tied to his understanding of Jean Cocteau as simply "a remarkable old show-off" (*New York Times*, 10 April 1962, p. 48.

teau came to equate his invisibility with his previously outlined demands for "elegance," saying:

> Invisibility seems to me a "sine qua non" of elegance. Elegance ceases to exist once it is noticed.[48]

Second, in terms of the relationship between the artist and his works, Cocteau came to view the dichotomy of the visible versus the invisible as synonyms for life and death. The poet must die and become invisible before his creations can properly live and their inner life ultimately grow visible. In the words of Francis Steegmuller:

> One portion of his meaning is that the poet's poetry must speak for itself; the poet must disappear. That is, the poet's "inner" life must disappear into the myth image of the verse. . . .[49]

Thus, in a rather intriguing manner, Cocteau seems to link his code of invisibility not only to the previously discussed poetic discipline of "elegance consists in not astonishing," but also to the ever-present question of the poet's "death."

For Cocteau, the rapport between his invisibility and his marked preoccupation with death (as noted in the two preceding portions of this chapter) seems very intimate. When speaking of the effects of opium—perhaps the common denominator between these two facets of his life—in his *Lettre à Maritain*, Cocteau states:

> The Chinese smoke in order to draw near to their dead. Invisibility comes from a motionless speed, from speed in its pure form. If the dead diminish ever so slightly their speed, a zone for encounter is formed.[50]

The dead are invisible. Invisibility comes from a motionless speed. Opium bestows upon the user a speed of similar nature so that he may become, partially at least, invisible and approach the dead through a "zone of encounter." One may read into Cocteau's analogy a number of varying interpretations according to the varying definitions of such terms as *invisible, dead,* and *speed.* One such analysis links this quotation to the two preceding ones. That is to say, Cocteau is once again referring to the methodological invisibility of his

---

48. Cocteau, Steegmuller's *Cocteau*, p. 4.
49. Ibid., p. 5.
50. Cocteau, *The Journals of Jean Cocteau*, p. 178.

technical productions—their "motionless speed"—and the fact that this invisibility is a necessary by-product of "elegance." Hence, to approach the "dead" (that is, the author and his intent), one must somehow become able to bridge this "zone for encounter": and opium allows for this very passage, due to its attributes of time and space alteration. In this manner, the normally invisible work becomes visible and the dead become, temporarily at least, living within the mind of the viewer. It is through this mechanism that Cocteau's communication via his works would be fulfilled, without his overt presence and without the risk of his social identity becoming confused with the message of his creation.

A further indication of the intertwined meanings of invisibility and death for Cocteau can be drawn from his numerous plays and films featuring various personifications of Death. Each figure portraying Death is "invisible" in nature; that is, their domain is not strictly of the physical world. They walk to and fro through mirrors and seem masters of both realms of the natural and the spiritual. Eva Kushner, in her brillant work entitled *Le Mythe d'Orphée,* observes:

> Here, Cocteau designates the spiritual profundity of Death. If death was only the coarsely carnal thing that one normally associates with the name, if it were only "visible," it would not be supernatural. . . . But the reality of death isn't only physical in nature. It is also invisible. . . ." It's actions are imperceptible to the naked eye. There are the living who are dead and the dead who are alive.[51]

Thus, a corollary definition to Cocteau's theme of the visible versus the invisible could include not only his problem of public credibility versus personal sincerity or the invisible "elegance" of his actual technical presentations, but also the entire cosmos of the Marvelous as dictated through the poet's art versus the mundane, everyday reality of scepticism and unshakable Cartesian empiricism everywhere prevalent in the rank and file of society's art lovers.

Whatever the case, Cocteau's sacred "invisibility" became for him more than a mere consolation or a fascinating piece of poetic abstraction; he subsequently came to regard it as a necessary part of his identity as a poet. Perhaps rationalizing the role in which his self-professed "invisibility" relates to his role as a poet, Cocteau came to

---

51. Eva Kushner, *Le Mythe d'Orphée dans la Littérature Française Contemporaine* (Paris: A. G. Nizet Publishers, 1961), p. 176.

consider its loss as an unwanted, indeed unthinkable, eventuality. In a self-made proverb to young poets, Cocteau would state:

> Don't call attention to inaccuracies printed about you. Such things are our protection.[52]

To grow gradually "visible" became, for Cocteau, synonymous with death—that is to say, becoming understood and systematically losing the sense of discovery inherent in the experiencing of his works. Down deep, it seems that Cocteau was mortally afraid of becoming passé. According to him, most great poets are, while they are alive, invisible to their respective societies. It is only after their (final) deaths that they and their works gradually become "visible" to their viewers. He explains:

> The true masters are "invisible." That makes sense, nobody wants the fashions to change, everybody is used to the status quo. Today Rimbaud is "visible," and it's my turn to be "invisible."[53]

And, again, in conversation with Claude Mauriac and André Gide, Cocteau is quick to point out:

> The true fame is, after all, when judgment ends, when visible and invisible are lashed together and the public does not acclaim the show, but the idea derived from it.[54]

Thus, Cocteau seems resigned, though rather happily so, to being, at least for the moment, "invisible" to his contemporary public. To be famous, for him, does not necessarily mean to be understood. Forever an optimist, however, Cocteau profits from his public's unawareness by emphasizing the fact that he can, from this vantage point, be *discovered*.

> Famous doesn't mean well known. To be famous and unknown permits one to be *discovered*. The remote audiences which know only my name and a few rumours about me go to see my films which, in spite of the dialogue, are a kind of Esperanto by virtue of the visual style . . . the style of images.[55]

The ideal is to be famous, unknown, and discovered.[56]

---

52. Cocteau, *The Hand of a Stranger*, p. 168.
53. Claude Mauriac, *Conversations with André Gide*, trans. Michael Lebeck (New York: George Braziller Publishers, 1965); p. 61.
54. Ibid.
55. Fraigneau, *Cocteau on the Film*, pp 29–30.
56. Ibid., p. 51.

As a man and as a poet, Cocteau thus capsulizes his ideals into a meaningful trinity of renown, understanding, and discovery. For Cocteau, invisible and yet all too visible in his public's eye, these three ideals seem to epitomize effectively his desperate attempts to construct a favorable relationship between himself and his works and his public. According to the artist himself, it is his renown as a social (though not necessarily artistic) celebrity, as initially beneficial as it may seem, which is at the root of his problem of credibility. And it is perhaps as a direct result of this duality of audience perception that Cocteau finds himself understood on false grounds—a fate worse than mere lack of understanding. Hence, discovery of the true aspect of both author and work seems mandatory if the vicious cycle is to be broken. And, once this cycle is interrupted and the author's renown ceases to mislead his ultimate comprehension, then a deeper and more significant sense of discovery may be achieved through his creations—the discovery of the familiar, deep-seated mythical patterns and prototypes present within each human consciousness, and the capacity for poetic communication with the beyond.

Very much akin to the personalized theme of invisibility versus visibility throughout Cocteau's works and ideologies is the apparent contradiction of his "truthful lies." This phrase seems, at its origin, partially to incarnate a portion of Cocteau's feelings concerning his relationship to his public and, hence, merits some investigation. In reaction to a number of his critics who consider him a "cheat" and a "false poet," Cocteau wrote: "I am a lie which always tells the truth";[57] for the author, as a poet, a mouthpiece for the beyond, *is* a lie—he himself is definitely not a human manifestation of the words that pass through his lips. He is but a man divinely possessed. However, the essential truths hidden within the poet's messages should not be confused with the social identity of the carrier, as Cocteau believes has happened in his case.

In this position, then, the "liar-poet" seems to align himself with the characteristic posture of the clown—he who wears a mask for the benefit of an audience who would find it difficult to accept his truths without resorting to some manner of disguise to ease that assimilation. Like a clown, Cocteau feels himself to be a walking, somewhat tragic incarnation of the dichotomy between what he is and what he is seen to be. He is seen as an entertaining and sometimes even com-

---

57. Cocteau, *Professional Secrets*, p. 104.

ical performer, doing his magic tricks upon the public pedestal, whereas what he *is*, behind the mask, is not revealed by his outward appearance.

He is a desperately serious artist, eternally misunderstood by those who fail to see beyond the greasepaint and the rouge of his "act." He is a lie, yet, through him, one may come to see truth—if one is able to see. He is altogether visible to the applauding gallery, yet that which remains invisible to his audience remains of utmost importance to him. Wallace Fowlie observes of Cocteau:

> It has been difficult for Cocteau's public to realize that his agility and his brio are only masks, and that his works, rather than being feats or artifices, are serious projects related to the great problems of the poet and human destiny. . . . Such a phrase as "true lies" describes the act of the clown who disguises his heart of a man.[58]

Thus, it seems that Cocteau willingly accepts the mantle of falsehood in order that his audience may come to believe in at least the outward aspect of his true identity and that of his presentation—in the hope that ultimately, via this partial belief, the inner truths of his "messages" may come to light and also be believed.

This strange and perhaps rationalized ethic of "lies for the sake of credibility" may be clarified a bit through the successive consideration of two of Cocteau's supporting philosophic premises. First of all, and again utilizing the image of the circus clown, Cocteau states that the public generally seems to prefer unreality to reality and easily understood falsehoods to confusing truths. From his *Essay of Indirect Criticism* he elaborates: "Falsehood is the only art form approved of by the general public, which instinctively prefers it to reality."[59] And, further, Cocteau seems to think that the general public is more easily able to *believe* in falsehood (due to its lack of complexity) than in the oftentimes unwieldy truth. In his *Lettre à Jacques Maritain* he attests: "The honest man is never believed."[60]

Second, Cocteau directly compares this affinity of the public toward the false and the unreal with the general role of *myth* as previously discussed—that is to say, a fiction conceived so as to ease

---

58. Cocteau, *The Journals of Jean Cocteau*, pp. 27–28.
59. Cocteau, *The Hand of a Stranger*, p. 2.
60. Jean Cocteau, *Lettre à Maritain* (Paris: Editions Stock, 1926), p. 12.

the digestion of a much larger truth or an otherwise inexplicable real phenomenon. He explains:

> Falsity . . . is akin to the birth of myths. In myths man seeks refuge. . . . Incapable of deep penetration of himself, he assumes a mask. . . . On a small scale, he mimics the painters whom he charges with madness. . . .[61]

As a result of these two convictions, it seems evident that Cocteau feels that, in order to communicate effectively with his public, he must present his poetry in a form most appropriate to the nature of his audience. And since he believes that the public instinctively prefers unreality to reality, myth to fact, and fiction to nonfiction, he accordingly cloaks his poetic truths in this regalia of "lies." This, he ironically affirms, insures the believability of his art and the first stepping-stone toward an eventual poetic communication.

But what also seems obvious in Cocteau's methodical explanation of his "truthful lies" is a certain measure of reproach and condemnation of those who criticize him. In shifting the blame away from himself, Cocteau redirects the public's very criticism against *themselves* and, in so doing, justifies his own motives and methods. A certain radio monologue written by Cocteau for Jean Marais illustrates this turnabout very aptly. Entitled "Le Menteur" ("The Liar"), the speaker (obviously a *porte-parole* for Cocteau himself) confesses that he is a liar and feels both fear and hatred for those who try to find him out. Through his confession of this crime, the speaker has caused his listeners to assume the role of judges. Then, attacking them, the speaker accuses these judges of occasionally lying and disqualifies them through hypocrisy. As a finale, he then says that he was only pretending to confess his lies, in order that he might bring to light the lies of his supposed judges. In this manner, the speaker seems to epitomize a "lie that always tells the truth."[62]

In any event, Cocteau's notorious propensity for fabricating lies that somehow endeavor to illustrate his truths seems to bring into perspective his marked preoccupation with "wanting to be believed" by his public. But the question still remains: which is the cause and which is the effect? Does Cocteau *mythify* (his favorite term for this practice of creating falsehoods) *because* he wishes to be believed,

---

61. Cocteau, *The Hand of a Stranger*, p. 2.
62. A copy of "Le Menteur" is included in the text *Voix du Siècle*, Book 1, eds. Eunice C. Smith and John K. Savacool (New York: Harcourt, Brace, and World, 1960), pp. 18–23.

given the aforementioned falsity-loving disposition of his audience? Or does he conveniently lie as a *reaction* to his criticizing public, weaving tangled webs of excuse and self-proclaimed innocence? The truth of the matter is not readily apparent (which, somehow, does not seem surprising), and Cocteau's believability on this point does certainly appear oftentimes questionable.

It must not be forgotten that Cocteau was repeatedly proven to be highly inexact when it came to consistent, accurate reportage of the people and events of his life as portrayed in many of his so-called autobiographical essays and works.[63] It seems that he would edit or stretch the truth to suit his personal needs or intentionally omit a large amount of pertinent information in order to make a point. As Francis Steegmuller observes, Cocteau was more interested in weaving the fabric of what he liked to call "personal myth" than the conscientious and factual delineation of his "personal history"—and, according to the precepts of Aristotle, the fictions of myth are "poetically true." "But a lie, even one that tells the truth, implies a truth that is not told."[64] And so, if one is to try to reconstruct the life and ideas of Cocteau and the hidden "motives behind the madness," one should not rely strictly upon the word of the artist himself via his writings; a vast imagination such as his can not be expected to restrict itself from an occasional tampering with facts.

But, beyond the philosophic premise of his "truthful lies," why would Cocteau feel the need to falsify? And, further, did he even realize it when he did blatantly lie? According to one of his contemporaries, Claude Mauriac, it seems very possible that Cocteau was acutely ignorant of his own falsehoods. Mauriac explains:

> The truth automatically becomes false simply in passing through that conjurer. Does he know that he's lying? I don't believe it. Lying is inherent in his nature. He tells a lie as poetically and beautifully as a merle sings. . . . I believe he believes in his own stories. He is an actor, but he plays with real sincerity. . . .[65]

"He is an actor," Mauriac explains. And it is perhaps this aspect of Cocteau's identity that is at the true origin of his affinity for perjury. After all, it must not be considered lightly that Cocteau, throughout

---

63. For example: *Opium* (Paris: Editions Stock, 1930); *Portraits-Souvenirs, 1900–1914* (Paris: Editions Grasset, 1935); *La Difficulté d'Etre* (Monaco: Editions du Rocher, 1957); *The Hand of a Stranger (Journal d'un Inconnu)*.
64. Steegmuller, p. 6.
65. Mauriac, *Conversations with Gide*, p. 57.

his life, was heavily involved with and influenced by the theater. He
had faced many an audience and had played many a role upon this
stage of trickery and behind-the-scenes fraudulence. For what more
is the art of the theater actor than that of a lie? The actor's only truth
is that he must help—even force—his audience to believe in the mask
that he carries. The best actors are seemingly transformed into their
respective stage-selves as the spotlight turns their way; their true
identity is left in the wings. They *are,* heart and soul, that which
they are depicting. And thus seems the case with Cocteau. When
speaking of Barbette, the transvestite acrobat with whom Cocteau
felt a strange kinship, he says:

> Don't forget, we are in the magic light of the theatre, in this trick-
> factory where truth has no currency, where anything natural has
> no value, where the short are made tall and the tall short, where
> the only things that convince us are card tricks and sleights of
> hand of a difficulty unsuspected by the audience. . . . Barbette's
> effect is instinctively calculated. We must transpose it into our
> own domain and use it deliberately.[66]

"And use it deliberately," he urges. And, as is evidenced throughout
his life and works, Cocteau did use this "ethic of falsity" very deliberately—oftentimes, however, with detrimental results to his own
credibility in the face of his public and friends.

Thus, similar to a childlike naiveté, or a sort of uncorrupted amorality most often found in young children, Cocteau seemed to feel
most at home in a fantasized world where the differentiating characteristics of the true and the false were not separated by a concise,
clear-cut dividing line. They blended one into the other; they often
assumed each other's appearance to the spectator. And it seems, contrary to Cocteau's insistences, that his elaborate philosophical con-
structions regarding his "truthful lies" are but an added afterthought,
a rationalized, though clever, defense against his probing critics.

Which raises a question essential to the understanding of Cocteau's relationship to his public: did Cocteau *really* want his public
to *know* him, the "real" him, or not? After due consideration of these
most revealing realms of Cocteau's "personal mythology"—"invisibility" and "truthful lies"—it would seem that Cocteau wanted desperately for his public to know him; but only the "him" that
he wished them to know. He desired that his public would *believe in*

66. Cocteau, "Le Numero Barbette," *Professional Secrets,* p. 90.

and *love* Cocteau-the-Poet, and *respect* (though not *know*) Cocteau-the-Man. Similar to the Wizard of Oz, he wished that his identity could be known strictly via his enchanting creations, his powerful and magical images, his intriguing enigmas of meaning and his famed chef d'oeuvres. Yet, before Cocteau himself could fully believe in this self-proclaimed identity, his public must unquestioningly believe in it. And the cycle begins anew.

Within this framework, Stanley Kaufmann's comment of Cocteau's public identity seems, once more, terribly appropriate: "Jean Cocteau, the poet as self-conscious hero. . . ."[67]

E. Orphic Identity

As should seem quite evident through the three preceding portions of this chapter, the most predominant theme expressed throughout Cocteau's works and autobiographies was his incessant fixation upon *death*. To one extent or another, virtually all of his later poetic creations seem to be somehow correlated to this often figurative, often literal personal fascination. Some of his best collections of poems, like *La Crucifixion* (1946), are heavily oriented toward an expression of this theme. Numerous plays and novels throughout his life seem to carry with them varying exposés of the reality of different forms of death; to mention just a few, one might cite *Thomas l'Imposteur* (1923), *Orphée* (1927), *Antigone* (1928), *La Machine Infernale* (1934) and *Bacchus* (1952). Further, Cocteau's massive volumes of literary criticism and autobiographical essays inevitably seem to devote page upon page to elaborate discussions about relationships of death to the poet and his works. From *Le Coq et l'Arlequin* (1918) through *La Démarche d'un Poète* (1953), one may always find varying references of Cocteau's to the many figurative and literal aspects of death. Movies were no exception. A striking example of Cocteau's liaison with death occurs in his first film, *Le Sang d'un Poète* (1932), where the entire plot development seems only a pretext for an in-depth study of death versus the poet. This same theme was more fully developed in his film *Orphée* (1950), and carried to its ultimate expression in Cocteau's cinematic epitaph of *Le Testament d'Orphée* (1961), where the phoenixlike cycle of death and rebirth has become more than just a personal the-

---

67. Stanley Kaufmann, *A World on Film* (New York: Harper and Row, 1966), p. 258.

matic preference by the poet but, rather, a heraldic symbol delineating Jean Cocteau's entire life and his poetic legacy to mankind.

Concurrent with and perhaps because of Cocteau's growing fixation on death (which, as would be expected, increased with his age), the myth and personage of Orpheus grew to be of major importance to him. Starting with his first serious treatment of this theme in his play *Orphée* (1927), Cocteau increasingly turned to the myth of Orpheus when needing a concrete and universally known illustration depicting the many "deaths" that a poet must endure to materialize his artistic creations. In the scene, for example, where Orphée has been torn to pieces by Aglaonice and her Bacchantes, his trunkless head somehow survives and is being interrogated by the Commissioner of Police:

COMMISSIONER.   As you can tell me your place of birth, perhaps you'll no longer refuse to tell me your name. You're called. . . .
ORPHÉE'S HEAD. Jean.
COMMISSIONER.   Jean what?
ORPHÉE'S HEAD. Jean Cocteau.
COMMISSIONER.   Coc. . . .
ORPHÉE'S HEAD. C,O,C,T,E,A,U.[68]

Thus, Cocteau assumes, in the late twenties, what became symbolic for him throughout his life as a mythic prototype—the god of lyre, song, and poetry, Orpheus. In so doing, his motives seem at first glance to be twofold. First, Cocteau crystallizes his elaborate poetic philosophy into one publicly acceptable personification and, accordingly, renders it infinitely more comprehensible to the insufficiently "initiated." Second, he increases the level of his own credibility and acceptance by attaching himself to the image of a generally admired and respected mythical hero. Initially, Cocteau hoped that the public, through the process of association, would identify him and his works with that of the Greek myth of Orpheus. Ultimately, Cocteau desired that his public identity would become so sufficiently infused with that of Orphism, that the two would be indistinguishable from the mythic. Such motives, though perhaps not terribly unselfish or profound, correlate rather well with Cocteau's extremely tenuous relationship with his public. And, such being the case, Cocteau's wish

---

68. Jean Cocteau, *Orphée,* from *Five Plays,* trans. Carl Wildman, et al. (New York: Hill and Wang, 1961), p. 44.

to align himself with the myth of Orpheus, to assume the latter's heroic identity, is but an indication of a self-proclaimed, persecuted man's dream of how he would like to be known: for instance, a form of sublimated self-projection with a heavy touch of fantasy completing the portrait.

But to what extent *is* Cocteau's identification with Orpheus just another "lie?" And to what extent does Cocteau himself believe in his own Orphic nature? If one is to consider time as the major instrument toward an eventual dispersion of falsehood, then Cocteau's case grows more and more intriguing. Consider that he first delineated his mythic identity in 1925 in his play *Orphée;* then, twenty-five years later, his film *Orphée* (1950) carried a much-changed but still recognizable illustration of the same identity substitution; and, finally, in 1961, Cocteau designated as his cinematographic epitaph *Le Testament d'Orphée,* having as its plot an idealized recapitulation of Jean Cocteau's entire life and works! Thus, for over thirty-five years of his long life, Cocteau repeatedly referred to his poetic identity as being parallel, or even synonymous, with that of Orpheus! In such a light, this strange preoccupation hardly seems to constitute a mere passing poetic fancy or stand simply as one of Cocteau's many "tricks" to briefly draw attention to himself and his creations. On the contrary, this curious rapprochement between Cocteau and Orpheus harbors a much deeper significance, at least to Cocteau, since it lasted for so long and remained so close to him. And, in accordance with this supposition and the possibility that such an eventual clarification may shed some light on a heretofore obscure portion of Cocteau's identity and the manner in which he expressed that image in a number of his more autobiographical works, the poet's "orphic identity" seems to merit a much closer investigation.

But what seems to be of primary importance at the outset of such an investigation is a detailed exposé of the Orpheus figure to which Cocteau finds himself so attracted. At first glance, an inquiry such as this appears rather simple and would initially seem to involve very little complexity. However, as one faithfully pursues the nebulous identity of the Greek poet, Orpheus, a disturbing fact quickly becomes clear: there were *many* Orpheuses, each highly differing from the other. Ovid's *Metamorphoses* presents an Orpheus of an entirely different nature from the Orpheus interpreted during the Middle Ages as "Orpheus-Christus." Appollonius' *Argonautica* includes a version of Orpheus entirely ignored by Virgil in his *Georgics.* The Orpheus of ancient Alexandria (perhaps the origin of Ovid's and

Virgil's versions) seems to have been unknown to Hellenistic Greece. And the confusion accordingly builds.[69]

Paramount throughout is the unavoidable fact that a complete "original" version of the Orpheus myth does not exist, and the information about Orpheus from the earliest Greek art and literature is extremely fragmentary. Nevertheless, drawing from scholarly works and other related sources, a partial reconstruction of the "original" Orpheus as well as his many "forged" kindred is possible. As a result, one is able to identify the composite attributes of the particular "Orpheus" with which Jean Cocteau defined himself and his role as a modern poet.

The original Orpheus, as known by the Greeks, possessed a certain number of characteristics that have become fairly established and accepted by most modern historians. He was born in Thrace, the son of the Muse, Calliope, and the wine god, Oegrus. He was an incomparable musician and poet, charming nature with his lyre, and inspiring men with his verse. An Argonaut, he accompanied Jason in his quest for the Golden Fleece. He was also a priest of Dionysus and a religious prophet, but later abandoned that cult to become a worshipper of Apollo. He was a vegetarian and firmly opposed to violence (perhaps it was this facet of his beliefs that caused his initial rupture with the Dionysiac religious cult, which practiced massive irrational bloodshed). Later, Orpheus also became renowned for his journey to Hades to win back his slain wife, Eurydice, charming Death's very home with his poetry and song. His labor was wasted, however, for Eurydice's return to life carried with it one condition—that Orpheus, during the long, torturous trek to the above world, must not look back at his love who followed. Yet Orpheus forgot his pledge, looked, and Eurydice returned to the shadows. Orpheus also, perhaps as a result of his lost wife, was known to spurn women and to advocate homosexuality (some Greek historians credit Orpheus as

---

69. Many excellent studies have been done trying to alleviate the ambiguity surrounding this well-known myth. Foremost among these, and those which seem to go the furthest in clarifying the varying identities of Orpheus, must include W. K. C. Guthrie's *The Greeks and Their Gods* (Boston: Beacon Press, 1968); Elizabeth Sewell's *The Orphic Voice* (New Haven, Connecticut: Yale University Press, 1960); and especially John Block Friedman's recent publication of *Orpheus in the Middle Ages* (Cambridge, Mass.: Harvard University Press, 1970). These few books represent masterly efforts toward tracing the Orpheus myth from its mysterious origin to its present forms in modern literature and the arts. Eva Kushner's *Le Mythe d'Orphée dans la Littérature Française Contemporaine* (Paris: A. G. Nizet Publishers, 1961) has been particularly helpful with regard to Cocteau's unique brand of Orpheus and the manner in which many other modern French writers have used the Orphic myth in their works.

the source of the widespread beliefs in homosexual love prevalent in later Greece). The death of Orpheus was at the hands of the Thracian women, either due to their jealous anger or at the instigation of a shunned Dionysus or, as some accounts testify, because of the wrath of Venus who disapproved of his homosexual practices. Another explanation tells of how Orpheus was torn limb from limb by the Bacchantes because he revealed to man the secrets of the gods, very similar to the crime of Prometheus. Whatever the reason, Orpheus' head supposedly lived on, and was retrieved by the people of the isle of Lesbos, from the Thracian Sea, where it had been cast along with his lyre. It was enshrined and grew to be a famous oracle until, as some stories relate, Apollo intervened because of its unwanted intrusion upon and rivalry with his own oracle at Delphi. Orpheus was thus silenced for all time and was put into the heavens, along with his lyre, forming the constellation of Lyra, where he was to remain forever.

But there is another, much different Orpheus whose myth seems to have been prevalent during these ancient times as well. He is Orpheus the monotheist, and his origin may be traced to the religious scriptures of the Hellenistic Jews and, later, to the early Christians. This Orpheus is divested of most of his aforementioned "pagan" attributes and stands primarily as a prophet of Mosaic law. According to some Jewish and Christian Apologists, Orpheus traveled in his youth to Egypt where he became a devoted pupil of Moses. Though he professed Hellenic beliefs when he returned to his native land, his true religious convictions were directed toward the one true god of Moses. In his old age, he recounted his experiences to his son, Musaeus, advising him also to reject the Olympian gods and convert to monotheism. These dialogues were supposedly written down in the form of a testament—the document being "discovered" around 300 A.D. by Christian scholars. Due, undoubtedly, to its extreme usefulness in converting the "pagan" populations to Christianity, this "Testament of Orpheus" (its historical label) was never questioned as to its essential authenticity. Written in the style and language of Homer, it became to succeeding generations of Christians and Jews an unquestionable and genuine piece of documented history, strengthening their self-esteem and consolidating the antiquity of their religion. Orpheus, thus, became one of the first Mosaic prophets of monotheism and his myth was accordingly woven into the fabric of Christian dogma.

But still another portrait of Orpheus can be found if one looks to the funerary paintings and sculptures of late Roman times and the early Middle Ages. This is the image of Orpheus-Christus: a strange yet highly symbolic mixture of the pagan Orpheus and Christ. It would seem that the origin of this mysterious figure proceeds from the early Christian artisan's desire to depict Jesus in a manner befitting a catacomb fresco, sarcophagus, or tomb mosaic. Yet there was no pictorial record of the physical attributes of Christ. So the artisan "borrowed" the iconography of Orpheus to portray his savior—thus the birth of the figure of Orpheus-Christus. The apparent sacrilege was minimal, for Orpheus had already become a "purified" pagan myth due to his sanctification via the "Testament." And, further, there seemed to be an abundance of parallel characteristics between the two prophets in question. John Friedman, in his book *Orpheus in the Middle Ages* observes:

> There were, to be sure, other gods and heroes who had led souls up from the underworld—Hercules and Hermes come immediately to mind as pagan figures adapted by the early Christian artisans—but Orpheus, because of his peaceful nature, his power of composing discord through music and eloquence, and his tragic death at the hands of his followers, was perhaps the most appropriate and certainly the most long-lived of the pagan figures for Christ to be used in funerary art. Undoubtedly his association with Jesus helped to keep Orpheus alive during the early centuries of the Church.[70]

Thus, Orpheus came to assume the role of Christian psychopomp—he who bears the souls of all good men to heaven—and his identity as the priest of Dionysus and of Apollo, as the Argonaut, and as the bereaved spouse of Eurydice was replaced by his new role as a Christ-figure.

But what of the Orpheus who supposedly fathered the ancient religious cult of Orphism and who established the doctrine of mysticism through his Orphic poems? This, once again, represents another of the many faces of Orpheus to which Cocteau found himself drawn. But historians usually draw a great distinction between the mythic figure of Orpheus himself and this religious movement that borrowed the authority of his name. One major reason is the basic anachronism of time and place between the two. Orpheus the man appears as a dweller in Thrace during or before the time of Homer. The

---

70. John Friedman, *Orpheus in the Middle Ages* (Cambridge, Mass.: Harvard University Press, 1970), p. 39.

cult of Orphism belonged to a period of history closer to the sixth century, and was supposedly born in Athens and southern Italy. In any event, Orpheus was somehow chosen as the patron for this cult, and it would perhaps be interesting to cast a brief glance at Orphism's basic tenets of belief in order to clarify the reasons why Orpheus was chosen as its representative, mythical figurehead. The Orphics preached an essential immortality and divinity of the human soul and, further, believed that constant ritual purity was mandatory if that immortality were not to be forfeited. The former of these two beliefs was Dionysiac in nature—a mystic "Katharsis" of the human spirit with the beyond (as practiced by the Bacchantes in their frenzied ecstasy) that thus rendered the spirit immortal. The latter of these two beliefs seems essentially Apollonian—laying great importance on purity and strict ritual as a means for human salvation. Orphism then, as a religious doctrine, would seem to stand as a synthesis of these two religions devoted to Dionysus on the one hand and Apollo on the other. Basically eclectic, the Orphics welded into one meaningful dogma these many differing religious elements of their time and, by so doing, presented an altogether new, refreshing, and wholly credible outlook on the nature of man and his relation to the gods. Man had an afterlife but he also had a strict moral code by which he must devotedly live, or else pay the terrible consequences after his death. His soul would be judged and, according to its merits, would be assigned to a place of punishment or happiness. After the passing of a thousand years, however, his soul would be reincarnated to once again live an earthly existence and once again be judged. The reasons why Orpheus was adopted as the mythological originator of this special religious perspective seems almost self-evident. The early tradition of Orpheus as a "converted missionary" of Apollo in this homeland of Dionysus, and his subsequent death, would make his tale seem very appealing to a religious sect striving to synthesize the doctrines of these two opposing religions. His immortality and reincarnation would seem obvious, for he had ventured beyond the grave and had returned. His music and song were one of soothing peace, joy, and beauty—very appropriate to a religious belief in human divinity and preaching a fundamental optimism in man's fate. Orpheus' opposition to violence and his vegetarian diet afforded to Orphism a portion of their established ritual toward purity. But, perhaps most of all, Orpheus represented a godlike man who had become manlike god, and this factor of his legend must have had enormous influence in the decision of the Orphics to typecast Orpheus as their prophet.

But to which of these many identities of Orpheus did Jean Cocteau align himself? The answer to such a question can only be, at best, theoretical. But if one considers not only Cocteau's many varied references to the Orphic myth, but also the many meaningful concurrences between these Orphic legends and Cocteau's stated private, poetic philosophy, his social identity in the face of public criticism, and his apparent psychological need for a mythic prototype to exemplify his role as a poet, the solution seems unmistakable. To a certain measure, consciously or entirely by accident, Cocteau identifies himself with not one, but *all* of the aforementioned variations of the Orpheus myth! I shall examine why, and, at the same time, illustrate to some exetnt the specific reasons *why* Cocteau originally in 1925 selected the Orpheus myth (other than the obvious fact that Orpheus was a poet) for his extensive personal and artistic usage.

First of all, one needs to remember Cocteau's fascination with death. The reality of death, its literal as well as figurative forms, was of primary importance to Cocteau and the thematic direction of his works. Over and over again, as stated in the preceding pages of this chapter, Cocteau defined death in terms of his poetic philosophy. Cocteau designated as "death" the transit made by a poet from the outer reality of the everyday world to his interior realms of the beyond, where his "angel" resided. To be "inspired," the poet must "expire." Note the similarity with the Greek myth. A journey of a similar nature was made by the poet Orpheus when he ventured through Death's door in search of Eurydice. And it might be further argued that Eurydice's "expiration" (initial and final) was a necessary prerequisite to the "inspiration" of Orpheus and his later legendary accomplishments.

In any event, it seems highly probable that Cocteau's identification with the Orpheus myth is largely motivated by the similarity of their two "missions beyond death" and the fact that each stands as a go-between, bridging the here and the hereafter. In a letter to myself on this matter, Claude Pinoteau, the technical director of Cocteau's *Le Testament d'Orphée,* observes of this particular semblance:

> When I knew him there was already this identification [with Orpheus]. Primarily, of course, because Orphée was a poet and

that he descended to this disquieting "beyond" through that dark tunnel which leads to Hell. . . .[71]

A similar "death" is experienced by the *audiences* of both Cocteau and Orpheus. The latter charms the living things of Nature with his poetry and song, with the aid of his lyre. The former tries to achieve the same effect with his poetry of the cinema, using as his instrument the atmosphere of the Marvelous. Both let their audiences temporarily "die" and allow their spirits to be raised to a poetic union with the "beyond." In his social affiliations as well, Cocteau was repeatedly described as a "charmer" and an "enchanter." Apart from the effects of his works, in normal conversation Cocteau would weave unending webs of witty and self-sustaining dialogue, continuing sometimes for hours his delightful, effervescent, and intriguing stories. At a party given by Misia Sert, a close friend of Diaghilev, Cocteau was once described as:

> Frail and sharp-featured . . . it would have been hard to improve on his youthful good looks. Along with his charm he had a great wish to charm, and he was the most entertaining talker conceivable. His conversation was like fireworks. He had a rare distinction . . . he was irresistible.[72]

Cocteau's apparent desire to charm with his brilliant eloquence made for him many friends and admirers, but made him many enemies as well; he came to be known in some quarters, as Jean-Paul Sartre would put it, a "dangerous trickster." As much as one disliked Cocteau, however, one could not help but admire his oratory genius and his capacity for spellbinding his listeners. One of his most pointed critics, Claude Mauriac, has said of him after an evening's visit:

> We arrive about 6:30 at the Hotel Vatel where he has a room. . . . Cocteau starts talking [and] will continue until 1:00 A.M. without letting anyone else get a word in edgewise, with the same dash, the same overflowing spirits. . . . The Cocteau style remains ever the same, copious and dependent upon memory, as always in an orator of genius. Sometimes he will speak extemporaneously without knowing what he is going to say and it will come out as though he were reciting a part from memory . . . he will make

---

71. Letter to the author from Claude Pinoteau, technical director of Cocteau's *Le Testament d'Orphée*, 6 August 1971.
72. Sert, in Steegmuller, p. 71.

additions much in the same manner of an ancient poet embel-
lishing a myth every time he tells it.[73]

Thus, Cocteau, as an individual as well as a poet, resembles Orpheus
and the mythic hero's famed talent for enchantment. By removing
their capacity of self-consciousness and redirecting their innermost
thoughts toward a poetic communication with the beyond, Cocteau
endeavors to entrance his audience and induce a momentary "death"
in their realization of the earthly world and its habitual harshness.

In addition to Cocteau's use of the Orphic death as a metaphor
for the poet's inspiration and the poet's "mission" to humanity, this
theme can be equally well applied to Cocteau's many self-proclaimed
"deaths" at the hands of his critics. In this light, Cocteau seems to
see in the myth of Orpheus a perfect symbol for the suffering of the
modern poet at the hands of an uncompromising public. Torn apart
by the frenzied Bacchantes of literary and cinematic criticism, Cocteau considers himself somewhat of a martyr, in much the same role
as he views the original Orpheus. Due to their prophetlike teachings,
both Cocteau and Orpheus were unjustly "murdered" by those who
opposed religious and/or artistic "innovation." It is highly probable,
as well, that Cocteau profoundly realized and utilized to his own
purposes the compatibility between the myths, not only of Orpheus.
but also of Christ. As was previously noted, Cocteau saw in the crucifixion of Christ a perfect metaphor for the poet's suffering and condemnation. And, so it was, that Cocteau used the ancient Greek myth
of Orpheus as a means to the same end. Cocteau undoubtedly recognized the similarities between these two historic figures and found
that, by associating himself with both, their combined effects were
very harmonious indeed. In one measure, Cocteau assumed the role
not only of Orpheus or of Christ individually, but of *both*—as perhaps a self-proclaimed modernization of the Orpheus-Christus motif
of the Middle Ages. This assertion seems all the more strengthened
by the fact that the "original" Orpheus-Christus was typecast as the
Christian psychopomp—he who bore good men's souls to heaven.
Such an attribute fits quite nicely into Cocteau's stated definition of
his individual role as a poet—he who bears men's souls to Poetry. In
any event, the actual martyrdom of both Orpheus and Christ and
the figurative martyrdom of Cocteau by his critics would seem to
comprise one of these many "meaningful concurrences" that would
motivate Cocteau to identify himself as an essentially Orphic figure.

---

73. Mauriac, *Conversations with Gide*, pp. 54–55.

Thus, through successive consideration of just a few of Cocteau's many thematic "deaths," one can begin to see a definite pattern that would logically link his poetic philosophy with the mythic legend of Orpheus. Both poets "die" when they undertake their respective trips to the "beyond"; both are agents of a figurative and salutary "death" with respect to their public and peers; and both undergo a martyrdom as payment for their efforts. Yet the similarity does not end there. Although "death" is probably the most universally known theme connected with the Orpheus myth and the one that perhaps most influenced Cocteau in his eventual identification, there are also other aspects of Orpheus that seem significant to the consideration of this legend. These attributes of Orpheus, his many exploits, accomplishments, and great deeds—those not necessarily connected to either his journey to the underworld or to his climactic end—are also of great importance and seem to find their counterparts in the personality, philosophy, or creations of Cocteau.

Consider, for example, the return of Orpheus from the dominion of Hades—his Christ-like "resurrection" from the dead. Would not Jean Cocteau feel the striking similarity between this facet of the myth and his own post-opium returns to life? Consider also the Orpheus who was the reputed initiator of homosexualism in ancient Greece. Cocteau would most assuredly find in this portion of the myth a reflection of his own self. And, finally, consider Orpheus the priest, who forsook the savage cult of Dionysus to become a worshipper of Apollo, and in whose name the religious sect of Orphism was later founded. Cocteau was throughout his life a firm believer in the art of the poet as being synonymous with that of a priest, and the function of poetry with that of religion. Elaborating upon this belief, he once stated:

> That is why, despite the current opinion that art is a luxury, it continues its priestcraft and imposes its necessity by the mediation of those who receive the illumination.[74]

Given these feelings concerning the priestly nature of his craft, it is not surprising to find that Cocteau likened the religious transition of Orpheus to his own artistic transition: from that of the precocious, undisciplined dandy of his youth to the serious, patient, and dedicated poet and artist of his later years. And the semblance seems even more significant considering the fact that the religious trans-

---

74. Cocteau, *The Journals of Jean Cocteau*, p. 175.

figuration of Orpheus followed his journey to Hell and his loss of Eurydice; whereas Cocteau's metamorphosis was, in part, the direct result of his many tortured years of opium addiction and the successive loss of many of his most beloved friends. And finally, Orphism's doctrine of ritual purity to achieve immortality seems to find its counterpart in Cocteau's technical methodology that the poet believes to be a deciding factor in the eventual immortality of his works, and thus, of himself. With regard to this attention to "purity" in Cocteau's works, Neal Oxenhandler aptly observes:

> For Cocteau, poetry is not primarily a dramatic representation of experience. . . . He is definitely in the tradition of "pure" poets for whom poetry is an end in itself and for whom morality is essentially an aesthetic function. He insists in his poetry on purely verbal and syntactical manipulations. . . . These notions are summed up for him by the keywords of "purity" and "freedom," and it is these terms, above all, which characterize his conception of the poet.[75]

Thus, for Cocteau as well as for the Orphic priest, strict adherence to a search for purity is a necessary element toward an eventual mystic union with the beyond and a subsequent immortality.

And on the topic of immortality, one final likeness between Orpheus and Jean Cocteau may be drawn: that which links the "aftermath" of Orpheus to the "aftermath" of Cocteau as he foresaw it. According to legend, the severed head of Orpheus was enshrined and grew to be renowned in all countries as an oracle of the gods. And, later, when Apollo intervened and Orpheus finally "died," to be forever among the stars, his legend and myth grew in men's minds to consummate his earthly immortality for all time. With regard to the oracular nature of Orpheus, one has but to cast a glance at Cocteau's beliefs concerning the poet's "angelism" to find a precise modern equivalent to this facet of the Orpheus myth. For, according to Cocteau, the true poet is not the creator of his own destiny but, rather, is "at the orders of his night" and a mere servant of the "angel" who possesses him. The poet, then, is an oracle, speaking strange and mysterious messages from the beyond and, like Orpheus, stands as an intermediary between god and man. Further, Cocteau foresaw his own immortality, as perpetrated through the future of his creations;

---

75. Neal Oxenhandler, "Poetry in Three Films of Cocteau," *Yale French Studies,* no. 17 (New York: Dranes Corp., 1956) , pp. 14–15.

like Orpheus, he believed that as a poet he was destined to become mythicized within the minds of men and, like most great historical figures, he would approach the timelessness of the "forever-present." Furthermore, Cocteau was extremely aware of and concerned with the future evolution of his works with regard to his future audiences. Perhaps this facet of his artistic consciousness was a simple defense mechanism resulting from the fact that the public of his own time did not appear to understand him or what he was trying to do. Or perhaps this very sensitivity would constitute another of his many identity-links with Orpheus. For, as Elizabeth Sewell states in her study of *The Orphic Voice*:

> In the Orpheus story, myth is looking at itself. This is the reflection of myth in its own mirror. . . . Orpheus is poetry thinking about itself.[76]

Thus, according to Ms. Sewell, one aspect of the Orpheus myth is its characteristic pose of introspective self-consciousness—a pose not at all foreign to the psychology of Jean Cocteau. His lifelong mania of self-inspection, self-evaluation, and self-emulation appears to the "uninitiated" as blatant narcissism, and would seem to relate the artist more to that demigod peering into a reflecting pool than to the Orphic myth. One cannot argue the point. But the fact remains that Narcissus was not a *poet*, and it was primarily *because* Cocteau was so terribly concerned with his own identity (present and future) in the face of his poetic creations that he appears so unduly preoccupied with himself. It is the prospective immortality of his works, and of himself, that haunts him and drives him to the point where he would seem narcissistic. Explained a bit by Robert Phelps, he observes of Cocteau:

> It looks like narcissism—excessive, obsessive, unrelenting narcissism. In a way, it is. (A poet's strengths are inseparable from his weaknesses.) But it is also something more. For Cocteau believed (or trusted) that his own history was as emblematic as that of Orpheus, his own encounters as fatal as those of Oedipus, his own beloveds as heroic as Eurydice or Hippolytus. And just as we no longer have Orpheus' own poems, only his myth and the meanings we continue to read into it, so Cocteau implies that

---

76. Michael Grant, *The Myths of the Greeks and Romans* (New York: Mentor Books, 1962), p. 277.

his personal trajectory of suffering and choice may remain in human memory, and usable to human speculation, longer even than his created works of art.[77]

And, as Mr. Phelps continues to say, such an assumption on Cocteau's part seems at first inordinately childish—except for the unalterable fact that Cocteau's "semimythic presence in twentieth-century civilization" is already self-evident, and, on the basis of that realization, it would appear that Cocteau knew well indeed what would transpire in the world, as regards his "myth," after his body perished. For Cocteau, his narcissistic pose was more a sign of his intense awareness of his mythical identity than of unmitigated snobbishness or conceit. And it is as a by-product to this special awareness that Cocteau created his "emblematic" epitaph, *Le Testament d'Orphée*. In much the same way as the legend of Orpheus-the-monotheist was preserved through his respective "Testament," Cocteau left to mankind a sort of "living record" of his life, his deeds, and his very person through this, his last film; and left as well, perhaps, the most clear-cut portrait of his own Orphic identity of any of his autobiographical creations of his lifetime.

Hence, Cocteau's identification with the myth of Orpheus grew, it seems, not only from a few simple similarities surrounding a literal and/or figurative view of death. It developed, for Cocteau, from a veritable host of other intriguing and meaningful concurrences relating to his entire artistic vocabulary, his personal life-style, and the very manner in which he defined himself, his profession, and the nature of his literary, dramatic, and cinematographic legacy! He apparently realized that he was living within the fabric of what was to become, one day, a myth, and he proceeded to elaborate upon that precise theme to the extent that his own history would become the history of the poet, Orpheus, and he would be remembered as such. The possibility that he may have been a true modern-day incarnation of Orpheus must have undoubtedly occurred to him; but what is important toward a more complete understanding of Cocteau and his works is the fact that he *did identify* with the personage of this myth, and this identification did leave its mark and should, thus, be accounted for.

Having discussed the reasons why Cocteau would find the myth of Orpheus so very applicable to his own life and identity as a poet, it would be interesting to clarify how Cocteau originally "discovered"

---

77. Cocteau, *Professional Secrets*, p. 12.

Orpheus. Such an undertaking, however, requires much extrapolation and guesswork, for Cocteau apparently left no record, implied or otherwise, as to when or how he first came into contact with the Orpheus myth and saw in it a reflection of himself. Renowned for his verbosity, Cocteau's exclusion (or deletion) of this bit of pertinent information from his many autobiographical essays seems quite unlike him. But renowned as well for his eclecticism, perhaps he did not wish to credit another with something that was to become so much a part of him and his artistic genius. Whatever the case may be, a reconstruction of the exact "origin" of Cocteau's fixation on the Orpheus myth can be attempted only with the understanding that any conclusions must remain essentially theoretical in nature and are highly prone to argument.

There seems to be one individual author who plays a predominant role in Cocteau's eventual choice of Orpheus as his mythic prototype. One might cite many such writers of the late 1800s and early 1900s who may undoubtedly have had varying amounts of influence on Cocteau during his very impressionable youth or his spiritual crises during his young, opiated manhood, and, through each, one might fashion a hypothesis directly or indirectly related to Cocteau's preoccupation with his own poetic identity and the myth of Orpheus (Oscar Wilde, for example, whose *Picture of Dorian Gray* profoundly affected Cocteau). However, one writer, above all, seems to have been primarily responsible for Jean Cocteau's introduction to this mythic raw material out of which subsequently sprang Cocteau's unique personalized Orpheus and his corresponding theme of the poet's many successive deaths. This author was Rainer Maria Rilke.

Jean Cocteau never met Rainer Maria Rilke in person. However, it was in the year of 1912 that Cocteau, as a young poet, rented a room in the Hotel Biron where Auguste Rodin lived. His first realization of the existence of Rilke apparently occurred during his brief stay at this small hotel that was to one day become doubly famous for its historical clientele. As Cocteau explains in retrospect:

> In the evening, at the corner window of the hotel, I used to see a lamp light up. It was the lamp of Auguste Rodin's secretary, Monsieur Rilke. I believed I knew a great many things in those days, and I lived in the filthy ignorance of my pretentious youth. Success put me on the wrong track, and I did not know that there exists a kind of success worse than failure, a kind of failure worth all the success in the world. And I did not know that one day

the far-off friendship of Rainer Maria Rilke would console me
for having seen his lamplight without realizing it was signaling
me to come and burn my wings in it.[78]

And "burn" his wings" Cocteau subsequently did. For it was some
years later after his stay at the Hotel Biron that Cocteau was introduced (supposedly via Blaise Cendrars) to the poetic writings of
Rilke, which became at once his fascination and model of emulation.
Cocteau's respect for Rilke grew rapidly and it was not without an
immense amount of personal joy and pride that he tells of Rilke's
telegram to him in 1926 after the opening of his play *Orphée* in Ger-
many.

> Rilke knew of my play *Orphée,* produced in Berlin by Reinhardt
> and . . . he sent to Mme. K. this moving telegram: "Tell Jean Coc-
> teau that I love him. He is the only one whom poetry admits to
> the realm of myth, and he returns from its radiance aglow, as
> from a seashore.[79]

According to accurate documentation, however, the contents of
Rilke's telegram was "make Cocteau feel how warmly I admire
him. . . ," but the differing message à la Cocteau shows, once again,
to what extent he wanted and needed to be liked by his respected
peer, Rilke.

In any event, what seems of major import to this study is the fact
that Cocteau's play *Orphée* was completed around 1925 or 1926,
while Rilke's *Sonnets to Orpheus* were published in *1923.* A simple
coincidence? Perhaps, but it should not be forgotten that it was during these years of the early 1920s that Cocteau began to grow quite
heavily attracted to opium, and it was also during this period, the
summer of 1925, that he proclaimed, "I've finally found my personal
mythology," during his extensive convalescence and disintoxication
from this drug. As discussed in an earlier section, it was during these
difficult years following the crushing blow of his lost Radiguet that
Cocteau "found" his poetic metaphor of the "angel," (as depicted in
his poem "L'Ange Heurtebise") as well as his themes of "mirrors,
the doors through which Death comes and goes," and the image of
Christ symbolizing the lonely agony of the poet (via Jacques Maritain). But, as history records it, Rainer Marie Rilke had just published prior to this time two of his most famous works—the *Duino*

---

78. Cocteau, *Professional Secrets,* p. 58.
79. Cocteau, in Steegmuller, p. 42.

Elegies as well as his fifty-five *Sonnets to Orpheus*. Further, the most predominant image throughout the *Duino Elegies* is none other than the Christian image of the *angel*! Such repetitive coincidences of this sort do not seem to occur very often. Although Cocteau has never made mention of the true source of his inspiration for his personal vocabulary of "angelism" and "Orphic identity," it would seem, to all intents and purposes, that Rainer Marie Rilke had a large hand in sowing the seed that eventually germinated into the poem "L'Ange Heurtebise" and the play *Orphée,* Cocteau's first artistic manifestations of these two themes. Francis Steegmuller observes of this relationship between Rilke and Cocteau:

> Opium, inducing a half-dream state in the elevator, might be said in the absence of a better word to have "fertilized" Rilke's angels for Cocteau, producing "L'Ange Heurtebise," and it must have been in large part his awareness of the intense relevance of that poem to himself that induced him to follow it with a direct sequel . . . of "Orpheus and the inexplicable birth of poems."[80]

And, as regards a satellite theme of Cocteau's fixation on Orpheus, the theme of mirrors, one needs only to glance at "Sonnet #3," Part II of Rilke's *Sonnets to Orpheus* to find a very interesting and rather significant counterpart. Quoted here in part, it reads:

> Mirrors: still no one knowing has told what your essential nature is. You, entirely filled, as with holes of sieves, you, time's interstices.

> But the loveliest one will stay, till there to her withold cheeks the unbounded clear Narcissus forces his way at last.[81]

Such a meditation upon the "essential nature" of mirrors seems to recall that portion of Cocteau's life at Villefranche-sur-Mer during the height of his opium smoking when he would sit for hours on end, staring at his reflection in a mirror, deep in thought, and very much identifiable as a modern Narcissus.

In any event, it would definitely seem that Rainer Maria Rilke had an enormous influence in Cocteau's eventual identification with the myth of Orpheus. As one of the first to portray for Cocteau the

---

80. Steegmuller, p. 42.
81. Rainer Maria Rilke, *Sonnets to Orpheus,* trans. C. F. MacIntyre (Berkeley, Calif.: University of California Press, 1967), p. 61.

many intriguing facets of Orpheus and his orphic arts through his *Sonnets to Orpheus,* Rilke stands as a predominant, though quite unsung, figure very near to the origin of Cocteau's subsequent Orphic identity, as Cocteau came to express it in such works as his play *Orphée,* and his later films *Le Sang d'un Poète, Orphée,* and *Le Testament d'Orphée.*

In conclusion, then, the reasons and origins of Jean Cocteau's rather perplexing identification with the myth of Orpheus, as he expressed it in many of his plays, films, and autobiographical works, seems to proceed from many diverse sources—philosophical, methodological, historical, and psychological. Philosophically, Cocteau saw in the numerous aspects of the Orphic legend a perfect mythic incarnation of his profound and often difficult-to-illustrate poetic philosophy. The death and subsequent return to life of Orpheus, much like the celebrated myth of the phoenix, appealed to Cocteau and offered to him an admirable vehicle for expressing his own ideas concerning the identity of all true poets who must live precariously balanced between the life of this world and the reality of the next. Although such poets may die many deaths at the hands of their critics and contemporaries, they are reborn with every poetic creation and, accordingly, remain immortal in men's minds. Methodologically, Orpheus seemed to epitomize all that Cocteau would hope to achieve through his technical productions. Enchanting all who hear, Orpheus pierced the hard-shell exterior of humanity with his poetry and song, putting their souls at rest and opening their eyes to beauty. Cocteau wished to achieve the same effect through his dramatic, poetic, and cinematographic productions, and dubs as his "Orphic lyre" the Marvelous— this special atmosphere through which he hoped to enchant his audiences and communicate the visions of his poetic state. Historically, Cocteau saw in the myth of Orpheus a multitude of episodes reflecting his own personal life. Orpheus' renunciation of Dionysus and subsequent worship of Apollo, his famed homosexuality, his deprivation of and heroic search for his lost love (s) , and the basic religious doctrines of his namesake cult of Orphism, all seem, for Cocteau, to be mythic extensions of the many events of his own life. And finally, psychologically, Cocteau found manifest in Orpheus what he deemed to be his "mythic self"—his primordial spiritual ancestor with whom Cocteau could identify all that he was and would be after his body was no more. Through his identification with the myth of Orpheus, Cocteau was able to truly examine himself and his future after death via his literary, artistic, and cinematic legacy. In the words of the mythologist Michael Grant:

> Throughout the centuries, therefore, many (perhaps most?) poets have gained strength and even originality by drawing upon the accumulated artistic, mythological heritage. . . . It provides a framework, a basis of tales and events appealing to the great human affections, which enables and encourages the poet to find himself—in the image of the mythical situation he can concentrate his emotions, or set them in perspective.[82]

It was, thus, within the "mythical situation" of Orpheus that Jean Cocteau found himself. Portrayed as this ancient Greek demigod of poetry and resurrection, Cocteau found his mythic identity, as it will remain forever depicted and preserved on film in such works as *Le Sang d'un Poète, Orphée* and *Le Testament d'Orphée*.

---

82. Grant, p. 277.

Three Film Interpretations

A. Introduction

Within the preceding pages much has been said concerning the artistic and sociopsychological vocabulary of Jean Cocteau: man, poet, and legend. Many of the fundamental elements of his poetic philosophy and techniques of portrayal as well as his relationship to his times have been discussed at length, and, as illustrated in the previous portion of this study, many hypotheses have been drawn concerning his Orpheus-oriented identity.

This final section shall, utilizing the perspectives and vocabulary aids thus constructed, attempt to shed light upon three of Cocteau's most autobiographical and intensely hermetic film-poems: *Le Sang d'un Poète (The Blood of a Poet)*, *Orphée (Orpheus)*, and *Le Testament d'Orphée (The Testament of Orpheus)*.

This study, once again, does not profess to explain these film-poems, but seeks only to offer interesting footnotes in the light of what has already been discussed concerning Cocteau's Orphic self-projection in his works. It is hoped that, as a result of such an investigation and clarification, the narrative, traditional symbol-codes heretofore used for the evaluation and interpretation of Cocteau's film-poetry may be replaced by a truer and much more meaningful code that would offer a greater amount of insight into these three cinematic works.

B. Le Sang d'un Poète (1932)

In January of 1932, Jean Cocteau arose before a small audience in the Theatre du Vieux-Colombier and stated:

I wish to now give way to a form of myself which may seem obscure or trying, but which remains a thousand times more real than the one which you see before you at this moment.[1]

In so saying, the noted author and dramatist, Cocteau, introduced the opening-night performance of his first cinematic chef d'oeuvre entitled *Le Sang d'un Poète*.

From that evening of 1932 until the present day, *Le Sang d'un Poète* has shocked, moved, confused, frustrated, and excited audiences in Europe and America alike. Its strange and mysterious imagery, its dreamlike atmosphere, and its lack of conventional narrative-plot structure has elicited both praise and condemnation from film critics and movie-going publics the world over.[2]

However, while the notoriety of *Le Sang d'un Poète* has been great, the number of intelligent attempts at clarifying the film have been uncommonly few. Recognizing the imminently autobiographical nature of this film with respect to its creator, a few literary scholars have proceeded to gradually unveil many of its mysteries. Among the more comprehensive and illuminating of these studies are C. G. Wallis's interpretation,[3] an essay by John Peale Bishop,[4] and those contained within the text of such books as Neal Oxenhandler's *Scandal and Parade*,[5] Elizabeth Sprigge and Jean-Jacques Kihm's *Jean Cocteau: The Man and the Mirror*,[6] and a few other studies as yet untranslated from the original French.[7] These texts have been invaluable in creating a broad spectrum of interpretations of *Le Sang d'un Poète*, and none claim to have definitively "explained" the complex imagery or the many "messages" of this film poem. Yet each brings the viewer a bit closer to a state of "initiation" into Cocteau's magical world of heraldic enigmas.

It has oftentimes been said that *Le Sang d'un Poète* was a Surrealist film, in spite of Cocteau's repeated insistence that, during this period of his life, he was attached to no literary school of thought,

1. Jean Cocteau, *Two Screenplays: The Blood of a Poet, The Testament of Orpheus,* trans. Carol Martin-Sperry (Baltimore, Maryland: Penguin Books, 1968), p. 67.
2. Cf. film review of *Le Sang d'un Poète,* Harry T. Smith, "A Cocteau Concoction," *New York Times,* 3 November 1933, p. 23.
3. C. G. Wallis, "The Blood of a Poet," *Kenyon Review* 6, no. 1 (Winter 1944) : 25–42.
4. John Peale Bishop, *The Collected Essays of John Peale Bishop,* ed. Edmund Wilson (New York: Charles Scribner's Sons, 1948), pp. 222–26.
5. Neal Oxenhandler, *Scandal and Parade: Theatre of Jean Cocteau* (New Brunswick, New Jersey: Rutgers University Press, 1957), pp. 63–67.
6. Elizabeth Sprigge and Jean-Jacques Kihm, *Jean Cocteau: The Man and the Mirror* (New York: Coward-McCann, Inc., 1968), pp. 119–25.
7. *See* bibliography.

The poet (Enrico Rivero) sleeps after struggling in vain with the image of the mouth impressed upon his palm. (COURTESY OF RAYMOND ROHAUER.)

especially that of the Surrealists, whom he detested with a fury. The rivalry between Cocteau and the Surrealists, headed by the dictatorial André Breton, dates far back to the early twenties when Surrealism was in its infancy as a literary and artistic movement. It seems that Cocteau was originally invited to become a member of the Surrealists' very exclusive group, but he declined, perhaps disenchanted with their social revolutionary practices and their quasi-nihilistic artistic theories. Whatever the case, André Breton never forgot this "insult" and remained forever adamant in his uncompromising hatred for Cocteau. Accordingly, as time went by, it was almost always the Surrealists who were responsible for such pranks as interrupting Cocteau's theater productions, poison-pen letters to Cocteau via the local newspapers, and innumerable other incidents, all scheduled to torment Cocteau and destroy his public prestige as a writer.

The misunderstanding with regard to *Le Sang d'un Poète,* how-

ever, stems no doubt from the confusion with the film of Luis
Buñuel, *L'Age d'Or,* which was first shown during the same general
time as Cocteau's film and was, ironically enough, commissioned and
funded by the same Vicomte de Noailles. In any case, although the
times in Paris were ripe for the flourishing growth of similar avant-
garde literary and cinematic innovations, *Le Sang d'un Poète* owes
virtually nothing to the Surrealist movement; Cocteau remained very
firm in his rejection of André Breton and his cohorts. This film, furthermore, does not claim to recite and record the interior workings
of the dream (the theme so inherent in Surrealist ideology), although, from a strictly technical viewpoint, the "mechanism" of the
film is strangely reminiscent of the Surrealists' dreamworlds. The actions link themselves together almost as if they had a will and a life of
their own. Through idea-associations and familiar yet hieroglyphic
allegories, Cocteau plunges the viewer into the realm of what he likes
to call "half-sleep"—the sphere where the Marvelous becomes an everyday reality and the marble Goddess of Poetry becomes a living, if
vengeful, personality.

As for the actual subject matter of the film, the following excerpt
from René Gilson's excellent study seems to adequately raise the
questions that *Le Sang d'un Poète* tries to answer:

> Where does poetry come from? What is poetry? From which hid-
> den folds of the soul does it arise? What is a poet? *Le Sang d'un
> Poète* . . . is a first exploration, an initial speleological descent
> into the abyss of the "poetic condition" . . . a first attempt to re-
> spond to these questions.[8]

This film does not present a narrative plot: at least, not as one is accustomed to expect from the usual cinematic experience. The ad-
venture that is unveiled through a succession of truly astonishing images is an internal one. Indeed, there are many indications that Cocteau,
consciously or unconsciously, created this film as an "invisible" reflection
of his own identity as a poet, as he previously implied in his preface to
the film. Furthermore, in André Fraigneau's *Entretiens Autour du Cinematographie,* Cocteau states as his rationale in making *Le Sang d'un
Poète*:

> I wasn't thinking about making a film. I was merely trying to
> express myself through a medium which in the past had been in-

8. Gilson, p. 79.

accessible to poets. So much so that without being aware of it, I was portraying myself, which happens to all artists who use their models as mere pretexts.[9]

Or, again, in the soul-searching *La Difficulté d'Etre,* he states:

Le Sang d'un Poète is only a descent into oneself, a way of using the mechanism of the dream without sleeping, a crooked candle, often mysteriously blown out, carried about in the night of the human body. . . .[10]

Thus, from the outset, it seems important to realize that *Le Sang d'un Poète* is an intensely autobiographical film, and the many events, images, and ideas projected in the film are, in large measure, a reflection of their creator, Jean Cocteau.

The poet, seeking to rid himself of the living "wound" of the mouth on his hand, transfers it to a Grecian statue—which promptly comes to life and reproaches him. (COURTESY OF RAYMOND ROHAUER.)

9. Fraigneau, *Cocteau on the Film,* p. 60.
10. Jean Cocteau, *La Difficulté d'Etre* (Monaco: Editions du Rocher, 1957), p. 77.

For reasons of brevity, this study will neither recount the entire plot of the film word by word, nor devote long pages to the supposed explanation of Cocteau's private mythology. Rather, the four essential themes, or episodes, of the film will be briefly summarized, then each viewed through the interpretive perspective of Cocteau's "Orphic identity." It is hoped that a new and seemingly ignored dimension of Cocteau as he projects himself into his works will be thus recognized and clarified.

First Episode: "The Wounded Hand" or "The Scar of the Poet"

A factory chimney begins to crumble and Cocteau's voice announces: "While the cannons of Fontenoy thundered in the distance, a young man in a modest room. . . ." One sees a young man—he is a "poet." Cocteau defines this term in its largest sense—he who "creates." After having seen the star-shaped scar on the shoulder of the young man and the star on his belt, it becomes clear that the central "hero" or subject of the film is Jean Cocteau himself; for the five-pointed star was, for many years, used by Cocteau as his pseudonym in signing letters, autographs, and art works. The poet of the film is drawing a portrait, in much the same way as the author of the film is portraying himself through the film itself. Suddenly his face suggests horror—the portrait is alive (same double entendre) and the mouth begins to move. The poet tries to erase the image, but the mouth imprints itself, lips open, on the palm of his hand. A friend drops in to see the poet but, horrified at the sight, departs immediately: leaving the poet alone with his creation that has, ironically, become once again an intimate part of himself. He tries desperately to rid himself of this living emblem but he finds that he can do nothing. The mouth begins to make signs of love to the poet and soon he can not resist its suggestive invitations, which are tantalizing and arousing him beyond his endurance. Caressing his body, the mouth-infested hand excites the poet to a sexual climax and the scene terminates with the young poet asleep.

"The following morning" the poet is still asleep and the mouth, still imprinted upon his palm, seems to be dreaming and murmuring the confused monologue of the poet's unconscious. Suddenly the poet awakens and finds, standing mysteriously in his room, an ancient Grecian statue of a woman without arms. In order to rid himself of his living "wound," he presses it to the marble face of the statue that, thus able to talk, becomes alive. She reproaches him and the poet suddenly discovers that all the doors and windows of his room have disappeared and only one large mirror remains upon the wall. Thus ends the first episode.

Behind the final door of the "Hôtel des Folies-Dramatiques," the poet views the narcissism of a hermaphrodite. (COURTESY OF RAYMOND RO-HAUER.)

With regard to this first episode of *Le Sang d'un Poète,* many scholars of varying disciplines have discovered within tthese first few scenes multitudes of symbols; particularly in the light of Cocteau's admitted homosexuality. Whatever the case, the relationship of the poet-artist to his creation evidenced through this first episode seems to suggest the *initiation of the poet to the poetry within himself,* that is, the initial perception (if not acceptance) by the poet of his identity as defined by his art. The poet realizes how the nature of the bond that attaches him to his art—love—and, since his creations are but extensions of himself, he must love himself (or, at least, love this particular aspect of his total identity). It seems evident, then, why the living "wound" will not erase: from the poet's first recognizance of his true poetic identity, his subsequent destiny is inalterable. However, against all reason, the poet still believes himself the master of his life and refuses to accept the reality and responsibility of his new self; thus, he believes his triumph to be complete when he applies the mouth to the statue and it remains there. This action epitomizes the "mauvaise foi" (bad faith) of a poet who refuses to accept his own poetic identity. Instead of laboring to find his unique tools so that he can express his poetry, instead of shedding his life's blood to fashion a "just image" of this poetry, he turns his back on this new awareness and randomly utilizes an ancient, "dead" art form to exorcise this uncomfortable, almost parasitic, portion of himself.

This particular scene recalls an earlier Cocteau during the age prior to World War I, Radiguet, and opium: this age when Cocteau seemed "le Prince Frivole" of the swank Parisian salons. Attaching himself to the salon celebrities of the time, Cocteau "played" the young and precocious poet, basking in his youthful notoriety. This was the age of DeMax, of Diaghilev and Nijinsky and the Ballet Russe, of Picasso, Stravinsky, Proust, and Apollinaire. Much later, when Diaghilev's "astonish me!" philosophy ceded to Radiguet's "elegance consists in not astonishing!", and Cocteau ceased to consider poetry a "game," he realized that:

> Poetry is a religion without hope. In it the poet expends himself, knowing all the time a masterpiece is, after all, but a number to a performing dog on quicksand.[11]

And, as a result of such an understanding, Cocteau came to create this enigmatic film-poem of old versus new poetic identities, *Le Sang d'un Poète.*

Second Episode: "The Walls, Do They Have Ears?"
The poet searches the walls and tries to escape the now prisonlike room. The animated statue says to him:

> Do you believe that it's so simple to get rid of a wound, to close the mouth of a wound? There is only one way left. You must go through the mirror.[12]

And following instruction, the poet walks through the mirror and finds himself in a strange and unknown world. It is in a long hallway of the "Hôtel des Folies-Dramatiques" (Hotel of Dramatic Follies) where he successively explores four rooms through their keyholes, like a voyeur. He discovers behind the first door the death, rebirth, and again the

---

11. Jean Cocteau, *The Hand of a Stranger (Le Journal d'un Inconnu)*, trans. Alec Brown (London: Elek Books, 1956), p. 3.
12. Cocteau, *Two Screenplays,* p. 37.

death of a Mexican before a firing squad. Behind the second door he
views a "flying lesson," that is, a young girl chased into flight by an old
woman with a whip. He sees behind the third door an opium smoker
who, from his side, returns the poet's stare. And, finally, the poet peers
through the keyhole of the last door and discovers a hermaphrodite,
beneath whose loincloth are written the words, "Danger of Death."
At the end. of the hallway the poet is given a pistol and he commits
suicide. His blood flows from his head to his body and becomes a red
drape, as a laurel wreath appears on his head. Cocteau's voice is heard
"Glory forever!" The poet angers, tears off the robe and crown, and returns to his room via the mirror. Furious, he takes a hammer and begins to reduce the statue (the mouthpiece of his destiny) to rubble,
while a voice is heard: "By breaking statues . . . one risks becoming
one . . . oneself."[13]

In the second episode, the poet finds himself enclosed in a room
with no exit save that of the mirror. The destiny of the poet (personified
by the statue) obliges him to plunge "into" himself, in order to be
"mortally" aware of his true poetic identity. The mirror suggests no
other symbol than that of an instrument that reflects images. Thus, the
poet enters into himself by the gateway of his own image (the image,
moreover, as his public observes him—"behind the mirror" remains the
poet's secret, personal identity). Further, everything that the poet is to
experience behind the mirror is but a manifestation of a reality that is
deep within himself—an image of this interior world that he rejects in
order to remain temporally and spiritually "free." There he finds his
personalized, familiar myths, his many sources of inspiration, all of the
Christmas-cardlike phantoms of his past, present, and future selves.
Time, as such, does not exist in this ethereal dimension; the poet sees
what he will *become* as well as the elements of his *past* and *present*. He
is afforded an intimate glimpse of his impending fate. This entire confrontation takes place in the "Hôtel des Folies-Dramatiques," which,
once again, is Cocteau's ironic play on words.

The first of these rather bizarre images, that of the Mexican being
killed, reborn, and killed again, suggests the poet's past (and, perhaps,
the future of the hero). The death-rebirth theme, as discussed earlier,
is central to Cocteau's poetic philosophy as well as to his personal Orphic
identity. During this scene, the hero hears a voice: "Mexico, the trenches
of Vincennes, the boulevard Argo, and a hotel are all the same. . . ."

---

13. Cocteau, *Two Screenplays*, p. 38.

Bathed in blood and crowned in laurels, the poet's death and glory are celebrated. (COURTESY OF RAYMOND ROHAUER.)

That is to say, Death is universal and is present in any given location of the world. This scene, therefore, evokes a portion of the poet's destiny: to be a true poet, one must die, then be reborn, and then die again so that each time he creates he can become immortal through his art.

The second image, "flying lessons," seems to suggest the rapport between both the poet and his creations and the poet and his public. To make his works "fly," to attain the height of credibility where the unreal becomes real and the unbelievable becomes believable, the poet must make strenuous use of discipline (suggested by the image of the whip). And, once his poetic creations take on a life of their own, having finally achieved this height, they break the bonds that attach them to the poet and, now independent of his will, insult him (perhaps in the form of misinterpretations, misunderstandings, and the like). Also, from another viewpoint, this scene approximates the relationship between the poet and his uncompromising society. In this case, the roles are reversed, and the poet, high above the rest of humanity, is, nonetheless, threatened, accused, and suspected by an uncomprehending yet vengeful public. The gestures of the flying girl's insolence, in this case, expresses the poet's defiance before his critics who appear "too attached to the ground."

Behind the third door, the poet views an opium smoker. This image perhaps needs no commentary, especially for those who are familiar with Cocteau's life. But what seems interesting, from the viewpoint of Orphic identity, is that the Chinese opium smoker, just before the poet leaves him, also becomes a voyeur and returns the poet's stare through the keyhole. As a mirror reflects the exterior image, opium reflects the innermost image of those who partake of it. It is especially this singular quality of some objects—those that aid the poet to "see" himself—that lies at the origin of Cocteau's preoccupation with opium, mirrors, myths, and a host of other seemingly narcissistic fixations.

Behind the final door the poet sees a hermaphrodite reclining upon his bed. An extremely strange image, the hermaphrodite suggests a theme already inherent in an earlier portion of the film—the living mouth—and typifies the bond linking the poet to his poetry, that is, love. The necessarily self-loving poet is truly hermaphroditic, for his love is directed toward his "other self" deep within him. Further, the price of this love "prohibited" by society is demonstrated by the words "Danger of Death" beneath the hermaphrodite's loincloth (where, anatomically, the organs of love are located). The necessity for the poet to "die" in order to culminate his love affair is also inherent within this image, thus strengthening the argument of Cocteau's realization of the Orphic "deathly" nature of poetic creation.

As if echoing the logical conclusions of these thoughts, the poet is then handed a pistol, which he puts to his head and fires. Bathed in blood and crowned in laurels, the poet's "glory" is thus celebrated: "Glory forever!", whispers his Muse in triumph. However, the poet still resists this self-realization and, leaving this world of the Marvelous by way of the mirror, he returns to his room, grabs a hammer, and begins to destroy the "living" object seemingly responsible. Thus nearing the conclusion of this second episode, the poet furiously and exultingly demolishes the mysterious statue in order to retain his "liberty." But a voice of warning is simultaneously heard: "By breaking statues . . . one risks becoming one oneself. . . ."[14] That is to say, by refusing "antiquated" forms, by breaking tradition, and by revolting against the established norms of the art world, the poet renders himself immortal

---

14. Cocteau, *Two Screenplays*, p. 38.

as an "innovator" and thus prone, subsequently and ironically, to becoming himself the "norm" of the future.

The goddess of poetry (the poet's death) departs, having accomplished her task. (COURTESY OF RAYMOND ROHAUER.)

Third Episode: "The Snowball Fight"

And, inevitably, the first scene of this episode reveals a statue of the poet standing before a school in the city of Monthiers. The statue is slowly being obliterated by the snowballs of some students who are warring among themselves in front of the school. One of these students, Dargelos, strikes another to death who falls to the snow gushing blood. The author then recites a poem entitled "The Comrade," of which the following comprises the last few lines:

This is often how these blows
Leave school, making blood flow
These hard snowball blows
That a fleeting beauty gives to the heart.[15]

Thus ends the third episode.

---

15. Ibid., pp. 39–40.

In the third episode, as in the previous one, time no longer exists. The past and future of the poet find themselves juxtaposed in the same scene. The poet, refusing the "immortal glory" prophesized by his destiny, has become a manifestation of that end, a statue. Instead of remaining alive forever within the minds of men, the poet finds himself remembered in the form of a cold, unemotional marble bust—a soulless shell, a celebrity of the past whose essence, his poetry, has been bypassed and forgotten. This condition is worsened by the fact that the statue appears to be made only of snow: a gray, aged snow that the students utilize as "ammunition for their battle."[16] And soon, "there is hardly any of it left upon the pedestal."[17]

This scene seems also to recall Cocteau's youth at the school of Condorcet and the myth of Dargelos as portrayed in *Les Enfants Terribles*. These memories reinforce the concept, shared by Cocteau, that poetry is often conceived from childhood impressions and later reminiscences of those experiences. And those memories, reincarnated through the poet's creations, often unexpectedly turn against the poet and strike him to "death."

Dargelos, then, seems an incarnation of this "angelism" as previously discussed. That is to say, he represents, to a certain extent, this "disinterestedness, egotism, tender pity, cruelty, . . . and naive amorality" that Cocteau terms *angelic*. Hence, while breaking the statue of "dead forms" (in the exact manner that the poet himself had done earlier), this young poet is soon killed by his own love (Dargelos-poetry). Sacrificed in the name of poetry, and angelism, the boy falls to the ground, bleeding his life's blood.

Fourth Episode: "The Profanation of the Host"

The scene changes. One sees that the courtyard of the school has been transformed into the shape of a theater. Above, seated in boxseats, are spectators who, while socializing among themselves, pretend to be following the performance. In the center of the stage, adjacent to the fallen body of the boy, a card table stands. The poet (no longer a demolished statue) is dressed impeccably in evening attire and plays cards with a woman who highly resembles the Greek statue of the second episode and who seems to be playing her hand with the utmost indifference. Disconcerted with his cards, the poet squirms. His hand slowly slides from the table and takes from the pocket of the dead boy an ace

16. Cocteau, *Two Screenplays*, p. 40.
17. Ibid.

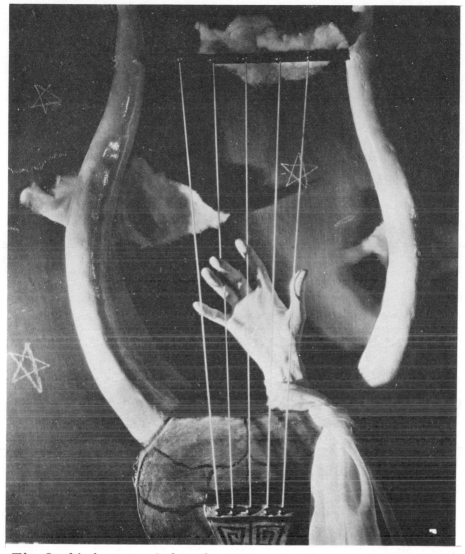

The Orphic lyre—symbol of the poet's quest. (COURTESY OF RAYMOND
ROHAUER.)

of hearts. However, his secretive strategy will not succeed because, at that
moment, the boy's guardian angel (a young, muscular black complete
with wings) appears and, retrieving the stolen card from the poet,
covers the boy with his body and makes him disappear. As the angel de-

parts, the woman speaks across the card table: "If you do not have the ace of hearts, my dear, you are a lost man."[18]

The heart of the poet beats desperately; the woman's stare is unmoving and glacial. The poet withdraws a pistol from his coat and shoots himself through the head. The spectators applaud. The woman becomes, once again, the living statue and the episode terminates with the image of the statue, a bull with a map of Europe imprinted upon its back, a lyre, and a world globe hanging in space. A voice is heard:

The road is long. . . .
The mortal boredom of immortality. . . .[19]

After which, the entire film ends with the image of the falling factory chimney, the completion of the same image that had originally begun the film.

In the final episode of *Le Sang d'un Poète,* the true denouement of the film, the inexorable destiny of the poet comes to pass. Again unconstrained by the element of time, this scene juxtaposes the past (the dead body of the boy) with the present (the poet who gambles his life at cards). The omnipresent theme of the poet versus his society is again made manifest through the not-too-attentive spectators. Cocteau, once more, portrays an uncaring, rather sadistic public, before whom he feels he must perform. The rapport between the poet and his poetry is allegorized in the form of a card game (illustrating, perhaps, the element of chance in all poetic creation): the stakes on the board? The poet's life, his spiritual freedom, as well as his physical well-being. In order for the poet's creations, his poetry, to live in its own right, the death of the poet is mandatory. There are two deaths inherent to this final scene; the first involves the already mentioned allegorical death of the author with respect to the ultimate acceptance of his works on their own strengths and weaknesses, without his presence and legendary notoriety interfering with their assimilation. The second death seems very real; the actual death of an author oftentimes projects his previously unnoticed works to lasting fame and artistic immortality.

The attempted theft of the ace of hearts by the poet may also, perhaps, be interpreted figuratively and allegorically. First of all, who is this ill-fated child? Is it truly Paul of *Les Enfants Terribles?* Or is it the poet himself, Cocteau, as a schoolboy? Or is it someone else; like all of

---

18. Ibid.
19. Ibid. p. 41.

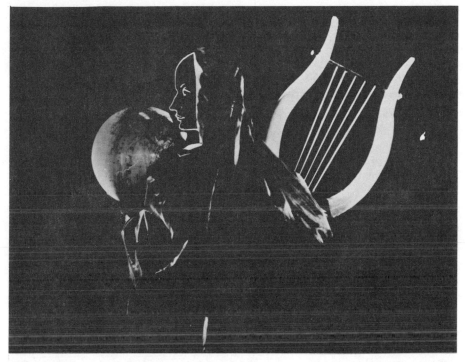

The goddess of poetry, carrying the scepters of her realm, leaves the company of man to dwell in her immortal resting place. (COURTESY OF RAYMOND ROHAUER.)

the young would-be poets with whom Cocteau became intimate during his long life and of whom Cocteau mysteriously witnessed the death one after the other? Perhaps all of these successive identities are merged within the image of the stricken boy, and, not the least of which, would be that of Raymond Radiquet, who exerted a massive influence on Cocteau's life and ideas. Soon after Radiquet's death, in 1923, Cocteau wrote a poem entitled "Ange Heurtebise," in which he makes mention of the death of Radiquet as the "ace which is missing from the game."[20] Hence, faced with his destiny and impending death (s), the poet tries to regain this ace of hearts from his past to avert his impending fate. However, almost as an ironic testament to the irreversability of time, the poet is discovered by the boy's guardian angel, his ace is taken away forever, and he is left alone. "You are a lost man. . . ," states the wom-

20. Sprigge and Kihm, p. 105.

an, seemingly referring to more than the outcome of the card game. With no escape, the poet promptly kills himself. The public befittingly applauds this "glorious gesture"—for, ironically enough, it is they who in the end triumph, in terms of what the poet "leaves to posterity" —and, then, they continue to gossip as before. Her task completed, the woman reassumes her statuelike appearance (her priestly vestments of marble) and, the Orphic cycle having made its full turn, the entire film draws slowly to a close. The final images characterize the inherent power, the "life," and the universality of the poetic state. Zeus, in the mythic form of a bull that carried away Europa, accompanies the goddess of poetry to their immortal resting place where, amidst her divine regalia of Orphic lyre and cartographer's globe, she seems to sleep. "The mortal boredom of immortality" seems to apply as equally well to the poet's plight as to the state or goddess of poetry and her earthly functions, particularly in the light of the double entendre, "mortal" (that is, the "deadly" rapport between poet and poetry and public).

"The mortal boredom of immortality." (COURTESY OF RAYMOND RO-HAUER.)

The final image of *Le Sang d'un Poète* concludes the tumbling down of the factory chimney that originally began the film. That is to say, all events occurring between the beginning and the conclusion of the film took place within a mere split second of the normal dimension of time. It seems, further, that this image is essentially one of destruction, of unequivocal obliteration. It has also oftentimes been pointed out that the falling tower seems allegorical to a phallic symbol, and its loss of its erective powers. Whatever the case, it is interesting to note that within this image and most of the actions of the plot, the relationships between the persons and/or object seem to fall into the classification of victor and victim, parasite and host, with either the loser's ultimate destruction or a subsequent complete reversal of roles. This atmosphere of constant combat and unsure eventualities seem to epitomize so much of what was near to Cocteau's role as poet. Fighting with self-discipline in order to reproduce the mot juste of his visions, fighting incessantly with his public critics who, Cocteau believed, sought to destroy him and his works, and oftentimes fighting *himself* in the rather disheartening warfare of searching his proper self-contained identity, all are "heroic" tests of strength between two or more protagonists. And it often seems difficult to know, in *Le Sang d'un Poète,* as well as in Cocteau's life, who eventually qualifies as victor and who as victim.

Thus, Jean Cocteau's first cinematic film-poem, *Le Sang d'un Poète,* seems a perfect example of an extensive elaboration by the author of his own poetic identity with regard to his public, his own creations, and himself as a "predestined" poet. One key to unlocking the many meaningful episodes presented within the text of this highly personal film-poem seems the concept of Cocteau's "Orphic identity." It is through the use of such a clarifying factor that Cocteau's rather complex "mythicized" cinematic vocabulary can be brought to the light of comprehension and, hence, carry the profound poetic messages of *Le Sang d'un Poète* to within the immediate grasp of an otherwise "uninitiated" audience.

But *Le Sang d'un Poète* stands as only the first of such Orphic self-projections by Cocteau via his film-poems of the cinema. Approximately eighteen years later, Cocteau was to again utilize his Tenth Muse for the same purpose, in *Orphée.* And, as a grand finale, he would, in 1959, begin to create a film-poem entitled *Le Testament d'Orphée* that would symbolize the final consummation of this three-part, personal film legacy.

C. Orphée (1950)

There is perhaps no other film created by Jean Cocteau that has attracted as much public acclaim and extensive literary analysis as his cinematic chef d'oeuvre of *Orphée*, completed in 1949. The following year, it won the First Prize at the International Film Festival in Venice and has, since its birth, been received the world over as one of the truly great films of the twentieth century.

For Cocteau, the film *Orphée* took up and reworked an old and dear theme first presented within the stage-production *Orphée* of 1925 and, further, within his first film, *Le Sang d'un Poète*, of 1932. As the author himself states in the preface of this film:

> The poet must die several times in order to be reborn. Twenty years ago I developed this theme in *The Blood of a Poet*. But there I played it with one finger, in *Orpheus* I have orchestrated it.[21]

But the film *Orphée* is neither a regurgitation of *Le Sang d'un Poète* nor a strict cinematic adaptation of the earlier one-act play of the same name. In recreating his cinematic version of *Orphée*, Cocteau, it must be said, changed more than he let remain. The plot, the imagery, the rhythm, the dialogue, and the very nature of the leading characters underwent massive transfigurations. For example, the play's sinister horse has been replaced by an enigmatic Rolls-Royce; Heurtebise (Death's emissary) is no longer a glazier but a chauffeur; black-clad motorcyclists rode to and fro accomplishing Death's silent orders; and the young poet Cégeste (to be reborn once more in *Le Testament d'Orphée* at a later date) is added to the drama of the plot. No longer a rather light-hearted, quasi-comical one-act play, the film *Orphée* stands as an extremely serious and highly profound cinematic masterpiece, achieving, perhaps better than any other of Cocteau's films, those poetic moments of the Marvelous of which he theorized so much.

As would naturally be expected, the quantity of scholastic comments and interpretations for the film *Orphée* are too numerous to cite extensively within this particular study. Virtually every text dealing with Jean Cocteau at all speaks at length of his film *Orphée* as one of his most important artistic creations. Aside from such biographical

---

21. Jean Cocteau, *Three Screenplays (L'Eternal Retour, Orphée, La Belle et La Bête)*, trans. Carol Martin-Sperry (New York: Grossman Publishers, 1972) , p. 188.

Author Jean Cocteau during the filming of Orphée. (COURTESY OF THE HAMMOND FILM LIBRARY, STATE UNIVERSITY OF N.Y., CORTLAND.)

studies, many film texts themselves include *Orphée* when speaking of modern European cinema. That is not to mention the many newspaper and magazine reviews written in both Europe and the United States when the film was first released.[22]

However, among the most comprehensive and detailed of such cinematic studies (published in English), one must include Margaret Crosland's *Jean Cocteau, A Biography;*[23] the brilliant, if verbose, study translated from the French entitled *Jean Cocteau* by René Gilson;[24] a very impressive article found in *Films and Filming* (October 1963) entitled "Orphée" and written by Raymond Durgnat;[25] Frederick Brown's rather gossipy study entitled *An Impersonation of Angels;*[26]

---

22. For a more complete listing, *see* bibliography.
23. Crosland, pp. 156–60.
24. Gilson, pp. 80–94.
25. Raymond Durgnat, "Orphée," *Films and Filming* 10 (October 1963) : 45–49.
26. Brown, pp. 256–66.

Francis Steegmuller's excellent work of *Cocteau: A Biography;*[27] Wallace Fowlie's *Jean Cocteau: The History of a Poet's Age;*[28] Elizabeth Sprigge and Jean-Jacques Kihm's *Jean Cocteau: The Man and the Mirror;*[29] André Fraigneau's *Cocteau* (translated by Donald Lehmkuhl),[30] and a veritable host of other fine and extremely helpful essays, books, and articles as yet untranslated from the original French.[31]

Originally, prior to his stage production of *Orphée* (1925), Cocteau had intended to create a play about Joseph and Mary; their trials and tribulations as parents of the Christ child, the gossip they endured as

Ruins of Saint Cyr, where Cocteau filmed Orpheus' passage through the "Zone". (COURTESY OF THE HAMMOND FILM LIBRARY, STATE UNIVERSITY OF N.Y., CORTLAND.)

27. Steegmuller, pp. 478–84.
28. Wallace Fowlie, *Jean Cocteau: The History of a Poet's Age* (Bloomington, Indiana: Indiana University Press, 1961) pp. 110–14.
29. Sprigge and Kihm, pp. 184–87.
30. André Fraigneau, *Cocteau*, trans. Donald Lehmkuhl (New York: Grove Press, 1961), pp. 99–104.
31. *See* bibliography.

a result of the inexplicable pregnancy, and their escape to Egypt. But, as Cocteau later asserts:

> The plot led to so many misapprehensions that I gave it up and substituted the Orphic theme, in which the inexplicable birth of poems would replace that of the Divine Child.[32]

Thus, Cocteau, even at this early date, drew a parallel between the life of Christ and that of Orpheus, with relation to the poet and his poetry. If the theme of Orpheus offered to Cocteau a much more feasible context in which he could portray the "inexplicable birth of poems" in the theater (and later on the screen), his feelings concerning the close proximity of these two myths of Orpheus and Christ should nonetheless be strongly noted.[33] And, such being the case, one should not be surprised to find within the text of the film *Orphée* numerous images and symbols of Christian ideology, particularly where they relate to Cocteau's conception of the persecuted poet and his vengeful public.

But to what extent *is* the Orpheus of Cocteau's film *Orphée* a cinematic incarnation of Cocteau himself? To what extent does he "identify" with the martyred hero of this film? If the perspective constructed by this study is to be deemed a valid one and if *Orphée* parallels the nature of *Le Sang d'un Poète* regarding their respective, raisons d'êtres, then one should be able to discern a very large amount of Cocteauean autobiography in this film.

And, indeed, one *does* recognize via the hero *Orphée* a cinematic personification of Cocteau. But such an observation is by no means astounding, for Cocteau has always readily admitted that his film *Orphée* was but another portrait of himself and his complex identity as a poet. In a letter to Mary Hoeck, he says of *Orphée*:

> Its moral is that the poet should be personally committed rather than be a follower of causes and parties. I think that this film is worthy of you and of our friendship. It is much less a film than it is myself—a kind of projection of things that are important to me.[34]

---

32. Jean Cocteau, *Professional Secrets*, ed. Robert Phelps, trans. Richard Howard (New York: Farrar, Straus, and Giroux, 1970), p. 260.
33. Cf., section of this study in previous chapter entitled "Orphic Identity."
34. Steegmuller, p. 479.

Thus, it is crucial to understand at the outset of any detailed investigation into *Orphée* that the hero of this film *is Jean Cocteau himself*, and everything that Orphée says, does, or experiences is, to a very large degree, a portrayal of the author's own life, ideas, and self-examinations.

Having clarified this relationship of the artist to his film, it would be interesting to examine the technical aspects of the filming of *Orphée*. Unlike *La Belle et la Bête* and *Le Testament d'Orphée*, a diarylike journal—relating chronologically the many days of filming on location and discussing the behind-the-scene activities of decor construction. script alterations, and the like—does not exist for the film *Orphée*. However, a few of the technical accomplishments of this film seem worthy of brief mention.

A rival young poet named Cégeste (Edouard Dermit) is killed by two mysterious motorcyclists, then transported to the eerie mansion of the Princesse (Maria Césares), who looks on. (COURTESY OF THE HAMMOND FILM LIBRARY, STATE UNIVERSITY OF N.Y., CORTLAND.)

Foremost among such technical "tricks," and perhaps the most famous, was Cocteau's use of a large vat of mercury for the filming of selective sequences where a close-up of a mirror was needed. Cocteau noted that, when penetrated, mercury does not ripple as water inevitably will, and, further, mercury reflects exterior images and yet does not reveal that which is thrust into it. Elaborating upon this technique, Cocteau says:

> The mirror into which Orphée dips his hands required about eight hundred weight of mercury. But there is nothing harder to come by than mercury, and nothing less simple to find than a tank big enough and strong enough to hold it. On top of that, it wouldn't have been safe to keep such a treasure in the Studio. So we had to do the shooting in one day, and we wasted a lot of time because it was almost impossible to get the caps off the drums in which the mercury had been delivered, and because the mercury itself was dirty. It had to be polished with chamois leather, like a silver dish. No sooner had one got that soft heavy surface clean than the impurities rose again and floated on top like oil stains. I thought I might be able to do without Jean Marais by putting the gloves on somebody else of his size. But when I tried I saw that hands were like a person, and we would have to have the actor himself. So he was sent for, and we spent the entire day, from seven in the morning till six in the evening, on that one shot.[35]

Another instance where Cocteau had to overcome the properties of the mirror occurred when the two motorcyclists walked nonchalantly through it (in actuality there was none there—just two adjacent rooms furnished identically) and yet when Jean Marais approached to do the same, he collided heavily against the glass. Cocteau explains his solution as follows:

> As there's only one shot, the motorcyclists couldn't have disappeared if there had been glass. Jean Marais knocked against an empty space and simulated the collision. I added the noise afterwards. The glass was put in only for the following shot, when Marais brushes against it and his cheek is flattened by the pressure.[36]

The grim motorcyclists themselves were conceived by Cocteau from the magazine *Paris-Match,* where he apparently saw a photograph of a postliberation funeral march. Leading the procession were two helmeted, dark-goggled and leather-jacketed motorcycle policemen.

35. Harry Geduld, *Filmmakers on Filmmaking* (Bloomington, Indiana: Indiana University Press, 1967), p. 151.
36. Ibid., p. 152.

Cégeste is resuscitated back to life and, recognizing the Princesse as Death, enters into her service. (COURTESY OF THE HAMMOND FILM LIBRARY, STATE UNIVERSITY OF N.Y., CORTLAND.)

A stroke of luck located for Cocteau two twin brothers, both of whom owned identical Indian motorcycles, to typecast for the role of Death's emissaries.

The "Zone," the no-man's-land between life and death that was found beyond Orphée's mirror was, in actuality, a desolate former military academy, bombed during the Second World War. These ruins were located near Versailles, at Saint Cyr.

But what seems to be of most importance, when speaking of the technical production of *Orphée,* is not the individual cinematic "tricks" themselves and how they made the normally impossible possible, or even the perfectly chosen locations, decors, and cast. It is, rather, the *combined effect* of all these "magical" elements that truly gives *Orphée* its flavor and its permanence as a classic. In *Orphée,* Cocteau achieves better than perhaps any of his other cinematic creations those heights of technical credibility and "unreal reality" that Cocteau chose to label

as the Marvelous, which is the first stepping-stone toward the communication of poetry.

As the title of the film suggests, *Orphée* recounts a modern-day tale
of Orpheus-the-poet, his trials and tribulations as an artist and as a
man walking perilously between the worlds of the present and of the
beyond. As Cocteau is quick to point out, the Orpheus of his film is
neither Orpheus the Argonaut nor Orpheus the priest of Dionysus,
nor is he the priest of Apollo. He is simply Orpheus the poet.

> In the film, Orpheus is not a great priest. He is a famous poet
> whose celebrity annoys what has come to be known as the avant-
> garde. In the film, the avant-garde play the role of the Bacchantes
> in the fable.[37]

The opening scene reveals Orphée defiantly visiting a café patron-
ized by these hostile writers of the avant-garde. Orphée catches sight
of the Princesse, a beautiful patroness of the avant-garde, trying to
calm a drunken young poet named Cégeste. A fight develops and her
chauffeur, Heurtebise, telephones for the police. They immediately
arrive, but Cégeste is run down by two mysterious, uniformed motorcyclists who drive on without stopping.

The Princesse orders Orphée to help her carry Cégeste into her
Rolls-Royce and to accompany them. Orphée soon realizes Cégeste is
dead but the car drives on into a strangely deserted part of the coun-
tryside and stops before an eerie mansion where Orphée, the Princesse,
and Heurtebise enter inside and Cégeste is carried in by the same two
unidentified motorcyclists. Cégeste is then resuscitated to "life" by the
Princesse and, recognizing her as "his death," the resurrected poet
enters into her service. The Princesse then leads Cégeste and her aides
through the mirror, but, when Orphée tries to follow them, the mirror
seems impenetrable and only a common mirror. He then loses consciousness.

Within these opening scenes of *Orpheé,* perhaps the most predominant theme expressed by Cocteau is his preoccupation with his own
identity as a poet in the face of criticism by his literary rivals. Cocteau
seemed especially sensitive to such criticism throughout his life, and
the opening scene at the Café des Poètes serves as a pretext for an extensive portrayal of just such a preoccupation. In one manner, Cocteau seems to be answering the taunts of his enemies and offering, via
Orphée, itself, a rebuttal to their condemnations.

---

37. Cocteau, *Three Screenplays*, p. 188.

Orpheus (Jean Marais) as he regains consciousness lying face down in a sandy landscape near a mirrorlike pool. (COURTESY OF THE HAMMOND FILM LIBRARY, STATE UNIVERSITY OF N.Y., CORTLAND.)

Consider, first, the opening series of dialogue between Orphée and an older, retired poet who seems Orpheé's only friend present in the Café des Poètes. The subject of their conversation is the hostility shown by the younger avant-garde poets toward Orphée:

The Man: Oh well. . . . I'm no longer in the rat race. I stopped writing twenty years ago. I had nothing new to offer. People respect my silence.

Orpheus: They probably think I have nothing new to offer and that a poet shouldn't become too famous. . . .

The Man: They don't like you very much. . . .

Orpheus: What you mean is that they hate me.[38]

---

38. Cocteau, *Three Screenplays*, p. 105.

Such a realization of the animosity of his peers for not being "radical" enough and allowing himself to grow too "famous," would seem on the part of Orphée a direct statement reflecting Jean Cocteau's exact feelings at this time in his life (approximately sixty years of age). Reacting violently to his exclusion from one of the more comprehensive anthologies of contemporary French literature of this time, Cocteau seems to invest Orphée's confrontation in the Café des Poètes with a significance much more pointed than it would normally appear. The editor of this particular anthology, Gaëtan Picon, reasoned that Cocteau was very much passé as a poet and, further, belonged to a "1920 climate which has nothing to do with us today."[39] It is not surprising, then, to find Orphée as a typecast figure reflecting Cocteau's thoughts concerning this facet of his audience appeal. But Cocteau did truly believe that the general public loved him, and that it was just the pedantic literary critics and rival artists who felt the need to attack him and his works. For, as the same dialogue continues, Orphée insists: "The public likes me."[40] Whereas his friend mercilessly points out: "Ah, but they're the only ones."[41]

It would appear, thus, that Orphée is expressing Cocteau's feelings on a number of different levels as regards his public image. First, Orphée-Cocteau concedes that he is loved by neither his rivals nor the academic scholars who devote their time trying to unravel his works and classify him as a writer. Second, Orphée-Cocteau is quick to add that his public, however, still admires and respects him and his many artistic creations. Orphée-Cocteau reacts to the former of these two assertions by casting a rather blunt qualitative judgment on the nature of his younger rivals' "art." Handed a copy of Cégeste's most recent publication, Orphée exclaims:

Orpheus (opening it): I see only blank pages.

The Man: It's called "Nudism."

Orpheus: That's ridiculous.[42]

An illustration of Orphée-Cocteau's second assertion, of his public's admiration, rapidly follows as Cégeste instigates a brawl and the police

39. Steegmuller, p. 480.
40. Cocteau, *Three Screenplays*, p. 106.
41. Ibid., p. 106.
42. Cocteau, *Three Screenplays*, p. 106.

*Night after night the Princesse appears (via the mirror) in Orpheus'
bedroom.* (COURTESY OF THE HAMMOND FILM LIBRARY, STATE UNIVER-
SITY OF N.Y., CORTLAND.)

are called in to quell the disturbance. Methodically demanding everyone's identity papers, the police approach the table where Orphée and
his friends are seated.

> First Policeman: Your papers. (*Orpheus takes his wallet from his
> pocket. The policeman looks at it and lifts his head.*) Ex-
> cuse me, sir, I didn't recognize you, yet my wife has photos
> of you all over the place.
>
> Orpheus: This gentleman is with me.
>
> First Policeman: Please accept my apologies . . . (*saluting*) Sir!
> (*He moves away.*) [43]

Thus, Cocteau seems to utilize Orphée's presence in the Café des
Poètes as another opportunity to express his own thoughts concerning

---

43. *Ibid.,* p. 108.

the relationship of himself and his works to his public. This relationship, for Cocteau, seems to stand as a polarization between those who love him and those who hate (although perhaps secretly envy) him and his art. One can not help but feel, however, that Cocteau is once again portraying himself as an unjustly persecuted martyr, and that the role of Orphée is, in this respect, strongly paralleled to that of Christ who experienced the same polarization of public reception before his crucifixion and subsequent resurrection from the dead. Such an observation seems all the more strengthened if considered in the light of the preceding chapter, where Cocteau's "Orphic identity" is related to his natural inclination to see himself as a Christ-like figure.

The latter portion of this first scene initiates the viewer to the elements of what will become the true drama of the film: the mysterious Princesse, her silent aide Heurtebise, the two ominous motorcyclists, and the now "dead" Cégeste. The Princesse, as following scenes will quickly determine, is a personification of "Death," or, at least, "Orphée's Death." In Cocteau's play of 1925 of the same name, one meets a similar incarnation of Death—an attractive woman dressed in elegant attire—but she carried no specific name. Why, then, does Cocteau choose to label the Death of his cinematic version as "Princesse?" One answer is offered via the research of Francis Steegmuller, who notes that, following Cocteau's dismissal by one of his closest female friends (Valentine Hugo), Cocteau sought comfort with the Comtesse de Noailles. This path of action soon proved to be a mistake, however, and Cocteau later came to call the Comtesse "Princess Fafner," after a legendary Norse ogre. Thus, Steegmuller points out, the inclusion of the "Princesse" in Orphée suggests a deepening of Cocteau's already rampant misogyny.

Such an explanation of the origin of Cocteau's "Princesse" is perhaps as feasible as any, but what of the other "changed" characters who bear very little resemblance to the play Orphée? Heurtebise, for example, who was a simple glazier (glass vendor) in the play, is now more closely associated with Death herself and the chauffeur of her Rolls-Royce; much the same as in the play, however, Heurtebise will subsequently fall in love with Orphée's wife. The Rolls itself, and its sinister radio, has replaced the horse; but both retain their capacities for mesmerizing the hero. And what of the inclusion of this new character, the poet Cégeste? And these fierce motorcyclists? And what happened to Death's "old" aides, Raphael and Azrael?

The answers to such questions are not immediately obvious and have

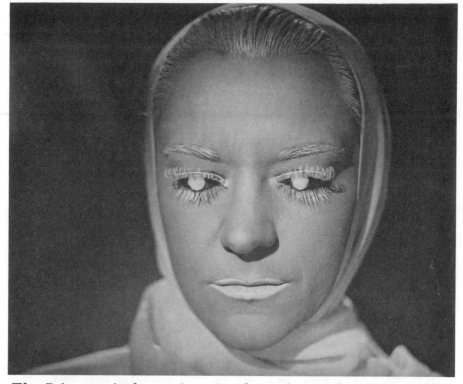

The Princesse, in her garb of Death, as she watches Orpheus sleep.
(COURTESY OF THE HAMMOND FILM LIBRARY, STATE UNIVERSITY OF N.Y.,
CORTLAND.)

been the subject of much debate since *Orphée's* first public showing.[44]
Cocteau casually dismisses such interrogations, saying that he merely
wanted to "modernize" the Orpheus myth and clothe it in a terminology understandable to the modern world. Further, Cocteau attests,
such questions are irrelevant to the total import of the film. He elaborates:

> Why is Orpheus' Death dressed in such or such a style? Why does
> she travel in a Rolls-Royce, why does Heurtebise appear and dis-
> appear at will in certain circumstances, while in others he abides
> by human rules? It is the eternal "why" that haunts all thinkers
> from Pascal to the most minor poet. . . . I wanted to touch on the
> most serious problems with a light hand, without philosophizing
> in a void. . . .

44. Cf., Robert Hammond, "The Mysteries of Orpheus," *Cinema Journal* 11 (Spring
1972) :26–33.

The closer one approaches to mystery, the more important it becomes to remain a realist. Automobile radios, code messages, short-wave broadcasts, power failures—such elements, familiar to all, make it possible for me to keep things down to earth.[45]

Following the death of his wife, Eurydice, Orpheus speaks with Heurtebise (François Perier) concerning the possibility of bringing her back.
(COURTESY OF THE HAMMOND FILM LIBRARY, STATE UNIVERSITY OF N.Y., CORTLAND.)

Thus, Cocteau dismisses such ponderings without offering any concrete solutions to such questions. Although the exact reasons for the presence of such individuals and props in *Orphée* may remain vague, their total effect is undeniable. In presenting a "modernization" of the Orpheus myth, Cocteau has ingeniously utilized and coordinated the elements of what Pauline Kael has described as the "new mythology." She observes:

The motorcyclists are part of a new mythology, they suggest images of our time: secret police . . . black heroes . . . the anony-

---

45. Steegmuller, p. 483.

mous and impersonal . . . agents of some unknown authority . . . executioners . . . visitors from outer space . . . the irrational. They are the men you can't reach and you can't deal with; they stand for sudden, shockingly accidental death.

Cocteau uses emblems and images of the then recent Nazi period and merges them with other, more primitive images of fear —as, indeed, they are merged in the modern consciousness. This gives the violence and mystery of the Orpheus story a kind of contemporaneity that, in other hands, might seem merely chic; but Cocteau's special gift was to raise chic to art.[46]

Hence, from the first major scene where one is introduced to the protagonists of *Orphée*, it seems crucial to understand that the question of "why are they as they are?" (particularly in comparison to Cocteau's previous play) is not at all as important as the questions of "*how* are they?" and "whom do they recall?" As Cocteau would undoubtedly affirm, it is necessary to *believe* rather than laboriously trying to understand his hidden motives and technical procedures that, by necessity, impede the communicative purpose of the film.

In the second major scene, Orphée comes to, lying in a sandy landscape, and is hailed by Heurtebise who then drives him home where Eurydice, Orphée's wife, is discussing the sudden disappearance of her husband and Cégeste with both the police and Aglaonice, leader of the League of Women, a friend of the avant-garde, and an old enemy of Orphée. Orphée pacifies the police, sends Aglaonice away, and becomes immediately obsessed with "poetic" transmissions from the radio of the Rolls-Royce, parked in his garage. Spurning Eurydice, Orphée offers her no explanation of his absence, while Heurtebise consoles her and tries to reassure her of Orphée's love. That night, and for several following nights, the Princesse appears (via the mirror) in Orphée's room and silently watches him sleep.

Aglaonice, meanwhile, accuses Orphée of complicity in Cégeste's death, but Orphée, indifferent to both Eurydice's emotional pleas and the counsel of Heurtebise, spends his time listening intently to the cryptic messages on the car radio. Eurydice, frantic, tries to go into town to appeal to Aglaonice but is promptly run down by the two motorcyclists. Orphée refuses to go to her aid. Heurtebise then carries her body to the bedroom where the Princesse has appeared with her new aide, Cégeste, who is broadcasting the radio messages that keep Orphée at the car's receiver in the garage. The Princesse performs her duties and leads Eurydice through the mirror to the underworld, but forgets one

---

46. Pauline Kael, *Kiss Kiss Bang Bang* (Boston: Little, Brown, and Company, 1968), p. 327.

of her rubber gloves—that part of her apparatus that enables one to pass through mirrors. Heurtebise remains behind, tells Orphée of his chance to reclaim his lost wife, and both, aided by the glove, pass into the mirror.

Within this second major portion of the film the plot begins to quickly unravel. One learns of Orphée's strange fascination with the beyond, his total indifference to his wife, and his hatred for Aglaonice, leader of the Bacchantes. The Princesse's attraction to Orphée becomes clear, as does Heurtebise's attraction to Eurydice. However, two particular themes seem predominant in this scene: the Cocteauean themes of poetic *inspiration* and his unique use of the *mirror*.

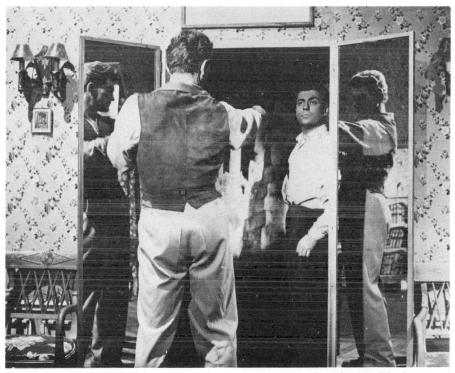

With the aid of a rubber glove that the Princesse had left behind, Heurtebise and Orpheus pass through the mirror. (COURTESY OF THE HAMMOND FILM LIBRARY, STATE UNIVERSITY OF N.Y., CORTLAND.)

As regards the individual theme of the poet's inspiration, Cocteau reiterates·in the preface to *Orphée*:

The theme of inspiration: one should say expiration rather than inspiration. That which we call inspiration comes from within us, from the darkness of our own night, not from outside, from a dif-

ferent so-called divine night. Everything starts to go wrong when
Orpheus ignores his own messages and agrees to accept messages
coming from outside. Orpheus is tricked by the messages that
come from Cegestius, not from the beyond.[47]

Much the same as the poet in *Le Sang d'un Poète*, Orphée initially accepts a false inspiration, this time transmitted through the radio of the
Rolls-Royce; such an inspiration can not be true, for the poet did not
"die" to achieve it. It is only after Orphée's many descents to the underworld and his many spiritual and physical deaths at the hands of
the Bacchantes and the Princesse that he can truly attain poetic inspiration and be reborn. Thus, through *Orphée*, Cocteau seems to have materialized all of his poetic doctrine concerning the mandatory Orphic
nature of the artist's inspiration, as previously discussed within an
earlier chapter of this study. Indeed, Orphée's entire plot and its very
raison d'être as a film-poem seems to hinge upon the same fundamental
questions that were answered in part through *Le Sang d'un Poète*:
"what is poetry?", "where does it come from?", and "what is a poet?" If,
according to René Gilson, *Le Sang d'un Poète* was the "initial speleo-
logical descent into the abyss of the poetic condition,"[48] then it must
be agreed that *Orphée* affords to the viewer of Cocteau a second such
exploration.

In addition to the theme of false versus true inspiration, which is,
perhaps, the most noteworthy thematic "message" of *Orphée*, one also
discovers a number of Cocteau's favorite items from his personalized
artistic mythology. One such item of major importance throughout
the film is the *mirror*: long established as one of Cocteau's most preferred images for portraying the doorway to the beyond. But what do
Cocteau's mirrors signify in terms of the underlying meaning of *Orphée*, and further, in terms of all of the preceding discussions aimed
at clarifying Cocteau's enigmatic film vocabulary? The answer seems
almost self-evident. In much the same way as Cocteau utilized the mirror in *Le Sang d'un Poète*, he continues to use it in the same manner
and for the same purpose. As the entrance and exit to the beyond, as
the "door where Death comes and goes," the mirror is an object that
reflects the image of those who stand before it. Thus, when plunging into
the mirror to seek his lost inspiration, the poet succeeds in penetrating
his own self. All that transpires behind the mirror in *Orphée*, to the
same extent as in *Le Sang d'un Poète*, is actually happening *within*

47. Cocteau, *Three Screenplays*, p. 188.
48. Gilson, p. 79.

the poet. And, further, the rubber gloves of *Orphée* that facilitate passage through the mirror seem reminiscent of Cocteau's admitted use of opium to facilitate this passage into himself. Hence, Cocteau's repeated use of the mirror seems to signify the outer physical shell of the poet—the shell that the poet must pass through in order to make contact with his interior "angel" and become inspired.

Heurtebise and Orpheus in the "Zone"—a no-man's-land between life and death. (COURTESY OF THE HAMMOND FILM LIBRARY, STATE UNIVERSITY OF N.Y., CORTLAND.)

Behind the mirror, Orphée and Heurtebise then traverse a "Zone" resembling the ruins of a city. Reaching an underworld tribunal at the furthest extent of the "Zone," they are called upon as witnesses to a trial where the Princesse stands as accused of killing Eurydice without orders. Her crime is "initiative" and her motive, love of Orphée. She and Orphée then express their mutual love for each other and Orphée, being a poet, is allowed to reclaim Eurydice on the condition that he never look at her. Heurtebise is allowed to return with them to facilitate their new life together.

The arrangement does not last long, however, and the next morning Orphée catches a glimpse of Eurydice in the rear-view mirror of the fatal Rolls-Royce. She promptly disappears. Simultaneously, Aglaonice and her friends burst into Orphée's home to avenge the death of Cégeste. Orphée is shot and the Bacchantes scatter as the police are held at bay by the two motorcyclists who carry off Orphée's body.

Beyond the Zone, the Princesse awaits impatiently for Orphée and Heurtebise. Embracing her love, Orphée, she then asks him if he will accept any ill treatment she cares to inflict upon him; Orphée immediately replies affirmatively and the Princesse orders Cégeste and Heurtebise to "kill" him.

Orphée awakens in his bed beside Eurydice. She remembers having a bad dream but Orphée feels that he has been inspired.

Beyond the mirror, however, Cégeste sadly watches as the Princesse and Heurtebise, guilty of insubordination, are marched off by the two motorcyclists to face a punishment "unimaginable to man."

Thus dramatically concludes *Orphée*. The Princesse and Heurtebise are punished for having loved Orphée and Eurydice and allowing that love to interfere with their assigned duties. And Orphée and Eurydice "live happily ever after."

Orphée has finally achieved true inspiration, but only after the many successive "deaths" of himself and Eurydice, his wife. Thus, Orphée comes to realize that he had been "tricked" by the transmissions of the radio in the Rolls-Royce and, forsaking this "found" inspiration to retrieve his lost wife. he subsequently experiences true poetic insight. The portrayal of this major theme in *Orphée* recalls one portion of Cocteau's poetic philosophy where he appropriately states:

> My method is simple: not to bother about poetry. It must come of its own accord. Merely whispering its name frightens it away.[49]

That is to say, by merely trying to "find" his inspiration, Orphée loses sight of its true nature, and consequently remains uninspired. As he eventually comes to realize, Orphée must undergo a number of "deaths," he must pass through this "Zone" (within himself) to make contact with the beyond. Inspiration, thus, stands as the outcome of a process in which the poet passes through a number of deaths to finally culminate his art in life—as illustrated by Orphée's "happy ending" where Eurydice and the poet are reunited in this world after their many "deathly" experiences in the beyond. It is only in life that the poet's death-pro-

---

49. Cocteau, *Professional Secrets*, p. 199.

duced inspiration can come to true fruition and become immortal
through artistic representation. Hence, the poet's "death" must die to
complete the cycle, and Cocteau befittingly concludes his film with Orphée's Death (the Princesse) sacrificing herself so that he may make
just such a resurrection to the living. And as the voice of Cocteau
affirms during this portion of the film: "The Death of the Poet must
sacrifice herself to make him immortal."[50]

*Heurtebise and Cégeste are called as witnesses before the tribunal of
the "Zone" where the Princesse is accused of killing Eurydice without
orders.* (COURTESY OF THE HAMMOND FILM LIBRARY, STATE UNIVERSITY
OF N.Y., CORTLAND.)

Another interesting item from Cocteau's personalized mythology
is found in this third portion of *Orphée* as well. It is this "Zone": a
no-man's-Land between life and death, between the reality of the
concrete world and the reality of the beyond. As Heurtebise conducts
Orphée through this strange realm of Limbo, Orphée asks where they
are. Heurtebise replies:

---
50. Cocteau, *Three Screenplays*, p. 182.

> Life takes a long time to die. This is the Zone. It consists of the
> memories of men and the ruins of their habits.[51]

That is to say, the journey of the poet to that "angel" residing deep
within him is one which is long and arduous. The poet can not merely close his eyes and instantly effect a communication with the beyond; it must develop slowly and the poet must pass through many
"levels" of himself before he finds what he is seeking. The "Zone,"
then, seems to be Cocteau's manner of illustrating the poet's transit
between his normal waking consciousness and that profound "poetic"
consciousness deep within him. Such a "Zone" could be likened to that
strange semireal world of half-sleep that everyone experiences just
before falling into complete slumber. In such a twilight state of mind,
various "forgotten" memories spring to life—in much the same way
as Cocteau's familiar image of the windowglass vendor (from the
play *Orphée,* 1925) is met by Orphée and Heurtebise as they traverse
the Zone. Orphée asks:

> Who are all these people wandering about? Are they alive?[52]

And Heurtebise calmly replies: "They think they are."[53]

Cocteau's "Zone," then, seems to represent that state of human
consciousness located between life and death. Life in this case, however, would be the spiritual life of the poet—his destination at the
far end of the Zone—and death would consist of the normal, unenlightened worldly consciousness of everyday living. It seems also interesting to note that Cocteau's conception of the "Zone" complements
very well his definition of the very role of the poet as a sort of go-between, bridging the here and the hereafter for the rest of humanity.
Thus, Cocteau unifies a bit the various elements of his poetic vocabulary, and, at the same time, provides his film *Orphée* with one of its
most intriguing and meaningful sequences of cinematic imagery.

Also evident within this concluding portion of *Orphée* are many
more instances of Cocteau's professed "public identity." One of the
most obvious, and thereby meriting the least clarification, is Orphée's
death at the hands of his avant-garde rivals, headed by his archenemy
Algaonice. Through this tumultuous sequence, Cocteau portrays once
again the frenzied hostility of some of some of his literary competitors

---

51. Ibid., p. 154.
52. Cocteau, *Three Screenplays,* p. 154.
53. Ibid., p. 154.

The Princesse makes her defense to the tribunal—her motive for the crime, love of Orpheus. (COURTESY OF THE HAMMOND FILM LIBRARY, STATE UNIVERSITY OF N.Y., CORTLAND.)

and their unfair and wholly unjustified attacks that "murder" him. It seems highly probable that Cocteau was genuinely hurt by such incursions, particularly when they originated from those whom he honestly liked or felt close to. Various individuals once very close to Cocteau were known, later on in their lives, to level bombastic assaults on him and their now-terminated friendships. Raymond Radiquet was one such example, and Claude Mauriac could be equally considered as another. Each, while young, had befriended Cocteau (Cocteau had been a very close friend of François Mauriac, Claude's father), but they proceeded to speak harshly of him as they grew older and became noted authors in their own right. In any event, the myth of Orphée seems to find its perfect modern counterpart via Cocteau's cinematic adaptation, for it was the former followers of Orphée (as a priest of Dionysus) who, in the end, were the cause of his death.

Another indication of Cocteau's preoccupation with his "judged" poetic identity occurs toward the middle of *Orphée*, where Orphée,

Heurtebise, and the Princesse are put on trial before the Tribunal of the Zone. The prosecution questions Orphée as to his occupation:

> First Judge: Profession?
> Orpheus: Poet.
> (*The Court Clerk stops writing and looks up.*)
> Clerk: His file says "writer."
> Orpheus: It's almost the same thing.
> Second Judge: There is no "almost" here. What do
>   you mean by "poet?"
> Orpheus: One who writes without being a writer.[54]

Utilizing a clever play upon words, Orphée-Cocteau justifies himself as a poet: he who writes without being a writer. Such a statement seems to accurately pinpoint the task of a poet, according to Cocteau. To write is not to create poetry that, by its very nature, transcends the mere paper and ink that poetry must take as its form to be communicated to mankind. Thus, Orphée-Cocteau once again defends his identity from that of a mere "writer" who knows nothing of the magical properties of language and who can not raise the human spirit to a union with the beyond as can a true poet.

A final indication of Cocteau's sensitivity to his critics occurs in the final closing moments of *Orphée*. The Princesse, having "sacrificed" herself for Orphée, and Heurtebise, having fallen in love with Eurydice, are both led off to face their superiors, to receive their respective punishments. Orphée and Eurydice are reunited in life, where Orphée finds himself strangely inspired. Concurrent with his new-found inspiration, Orphée also experiences an attitude change with regard to his wife; he now seems deeply in love with her and affords to her his utmost attention and affection. Asking Eurydice as to the health of the yet-to-be-born child, Eurydice replies:

> Eurydice:
>   He's kicking me. He punches me, too.
> Orpheus:
>   He will be as unbearable as his father.
> Eurydice:
>   You, unbearable?
> (*They kiss, laughing.*)
> Orpheus:
>   Many people find me unbearable.
> Eurydice:
>   You shouldn't complain, you are adored!

---

54. Cocteau, *Three Screenplays*, pp. 158–89.

Orpheus, having regained Eurydice (Marie Dea) but may not look at her, struggles to keep his part of the bargain—but the situation is to be short-lived. (COURTESY OF THE HAMMOND FILM LIBRARY, STATE UNIVERSITY OF N.Y., CORTLAND.)

Orpheus:
> And hated. . . .

Eurydice:
> That's just a form of love.[55]

Reminiscent of the opening scene, in the Café aux Poètes, where Orphée speaks of his being both loved and hated, this final passage once again touches upon the same theme. Such repeated references by Cocteau to the many facets of his public identity, using Orphée as his mouthpiece, seems to confirm the assertion that Cocteau was consciously striving to communicate this portion of himself, as well as many others, through his film *Orphée*.

There are a multitude of other very important themes within the

---

55. Cocteau, *Three Screenplays,* p. 186.

film *Orphée,* each representing to one degree or another the personality or beliefs of Cocteau. The contrast between Orphée's "love" for Eurydice (a woman) and his "love" for the Princesse (his Death and Muse), for example, could be discussed at length in terms of Cocteau's personal inclinations toward love. Heurtebise, for example, could be analyzed in terms of Cocteau's previously noted vocabulary of "angels." The element of time and its deformation in the film *Orphée,* for example, could be traced to the similar transformations of Time in *Le Sang d'un Poète,* and assumptions could accordingly be drawn concerning Cocteau's fascination with the elements of space and time and how he felt that the cinematograph is artistically superior to any other art form because of its capability to alter these two elements.

But one particular theme seems to outweigh all others, and seems

Shot to death in revenge for the slaying of Cégeste, Orpheus once more finds the Princesse awaiting him in the "Zone." They declare their ill-fated love for one another before she sends him back to life with Eurydice for a final time. (COURTESY OF THE HAMMOND FILM LIBRARY, STATE UNIVERSITY OF N.Y., CORTLAND.)

furthermore, to go hand in hand with Cocteau's meaningful portrayal of the poet's many deaths and his resulting poetic inspiration in *Orphée*. This is the theme of the inalterable destiny of the poet versus his capacities of free will: the will of the gods versus the desires of man. Very similar to the predominant "message" of *Le Sang d'un Poète*, Cocteau seems to once again typecast the poet as one whose fate is determined and who is destined for fame, like it or not. The poet is but an instrument toward the manifestation of Poetry that lives in the guise of the poet's creations. The poet is at the "orders of his night" and assumes the role of intermediary between man and the beyond. The poet's personal wants, needs, and cravings must be considered secondary to his primary function as an oracle, a chronicler of the mysteries of the unknown. When asked by Eurydice to rest himself, Orphée replies:

> Orpheus' Voice: My books won't write themselves, you know.
> Eurydice's Voice: Your books do write themselves.
> Orpheus: I help them. . . .[56]

To "help" his poetry achieve earthly portrayal is the poet's task, and his very identity is contained within that framework.

Perhaps the most remarkable and significant illustration of this particular theme within *Orphée* is the actual denouement of the entire film, when the Princesse "kills" Orphée, bringing him back to life, and heroically prepares to face her inevitable and terrible punishment for this crime. In effect, the Princesse, who is Orphée's Death, sacrifices her love for him, in favor of poetry and life. Such a climactic outcome of the poet's numerous "deaths" and visits to the underworld draws to mind a parallel circumstance experienced on a number of occasions by Cocteau. That is to say, each time that Cocteau, with or without the help of opium, "died" and journeyed to that realm of the beyond within himself, he was forced to reluctantly return to "life." Having found his inspiration, he was forced to reassume his normal waking consciousness in order to adequately portray his visions. By whom or what was he forced to make such a return? By the *Poetry* that was within him; by his "night" that demanded his services; by his inspiration itself that would not heed its host's personal inclinations or desires and was concerned only with its own incarnation through an art form. Perhaps Cocteau, like Orphée, would have preferred to remain forever in the domain of the beyond with his "love,"

---

56. Cocteau, *Three Screenplays*, p. 186.

but his destiny was not of that order. He would "die" many times, and each time he would return, be "resurrected" from the dead, be "reborn," to perform his worldly tasks in the name of his Muse. This particular cycle, as a very predominant theme of Cocteau's film *Orphée,* is once again a reflection of Cocteau's many-faceted "Orphic identity" and stands as a major illustration of how he projected this complex poetic identity through his works. Through *Orphée,* in the same manner as in *Le Sang d'un Poète,* Cocteau poses the problem of the poet's quest. And, in response to this problem, Cocteau echoes once again the same answers.

Awaking as from a dream, Orpheus and Eurydice discuss their new-found love and poetic inspiration—they can remember nothing of their experiences. (COURTESY OF THE HAMMOND FILM LIBRARY, STATE UNIVERSITY OF N.Y., CORTLAND.)

Cocteau's cinematic masterpiece of *Orphée,* then, is a film highly autobiographical in nature and reflects many of Cocteau's personal and poetic beliefs. As noted within the introduction of this chapter, Cocteau claims that, through *Orphée,* he "orchestrates" the same themes that he had "played clumsily" in *Le Sang d'un Poète* twenty years earlier. And, as seems evident through the investigations of *Orphée* presented within this chapter, those themes seem to almost invariably touch upon what one might term Cocteau's *Orphic identity*. But the cycle is not yet complete, and it is not until the year of 1959 that Cocteau would bring to culmination his prolonged cinematic self-portrait, terminating his three-part film legacy with his personalized epitaph of *Le Testament d'Orphée*.

D. Le Testament d'Orphée (1960)

In 1959, Jean Cocteau began to film what was to become his final cinematographic work, his last personalized film-poem, *Le Testament d'Orphée*. As the title suggests, this film, which so aptly completes his explorations of self begun in *Le Sang d'un Poète* and continued in *Orphée*, symbolizes the final few brush strokes toward an elaborate and enigmatic inner portrait of the author and must be considered, as he himself would explain, a lasting epitaph of his entire life, works, and self-examinations as a poet. Befittingly, Cocteau plays the leading role himself—a modern-day Orpheus, signaling an Orphic farewell to his "Tenth Muse" and embroidering once again into the fabric of that myth a poetic recapitulation of the "phoenixology" of a poet's true identity in the face of his creations, his judges, and his own self. As its subtitle *Le Testament* carries the warning, "Don't Ask Me Why," and Cocteau explains this choice as follows:

> This film is not, in the true sense of the word, a film, but rather it offered to me the only way in which I could portray objectively, sensitively and, I will say myself, in a familiar manner those things which I carry within me without really understanding them. . . .
>
> It's subtitle, "Don't Ask Me Why," signifies that I would be incapable of saying why I led, from one end to the other, an adventure which corresponds to none of the imperatives of the cinematograph.
>
> The only thing which I may state in confidence is that the cinematograph, through the possibilities which it offers in tampering with time and vanquishing its own narrow limits, is the only language suitable for bringing my night into the daylight and putting it on a table in the full sun.[57]

---

57. Roger Pillaudin, *Jean Cocteau Tourne Son Dernier Film* (Paris: La Table Ronde, 1960), p. 9.

Thus, *Le Testament d'Orphée* is an attempt by Cocteau to portray, once more, the workings of his "night" to which he remains but a humble and unquestioning servant. Intimidated by those who, he feels, will undoubtedly ask him for the "meaning" of *Le Testament*, Cocteau stipulates at the outset that he has no answers to any such questions. One feels led to wonder, however, whether Cocteau truly has no explanations or whether he is simply refusing to sacrifice the film's inherent "invisibility" to public interpretation. Whatever the case, *Le Testament d'Orphée* stands as a self-imposed, though quite inscrutable, personal monument to Jean Cocteau's poetic identity as he would like to have it known for all times.

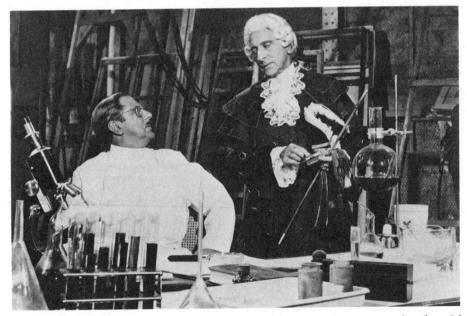

The poet (Jean Cocteau), lost in a space-time continuum, seeks the aid of the professor (Henry Crémieux). (COURTESY OF CONTEMPORARY FILMS /MC GRAW-HILL.)

Due perhaps to its comparative infancy as a recognized film, *Le Testament d'Orphée*, to date, has extremely few critical interpretations. Many studies dealing with Cocteau, particularly those written since 1960 or so, have mentioned this film, but extensive commentaries as to its content are rare.[58] However, an excellent and quite complete account of the technical aspects involved in the filming of *Le Testament* exists in the form of Roger Pillaudin's *Jean Cocteau Tourne Son Dernier Film*,[59] but remains as yet untranslated from the original French. Filled with numerous personal interviews with the case, accurate descriptions of set decors, and many significant insights into behind-the-scenes actions, Pillaudin's diarylike journal is an incomparable aid toward unveiling the many mysteries of *Le Testament d'Orphée*. And, as such, it stands alone, for there are virtually no other books in print that are devoted to the study of this film.

The "plot," as such, of *Le Testament* does not follow a traditional linear and logical pattern of drama. The events experienced by the poet within the film seem to take place, rather, within the "discontinuous" continuity of a dream sequence. The images seem set one against the other and proceed not through a patterned cause-effect relationship but, rather, through a "vertical" progression as prevalent in the disjointed imagery of a poetry reading. In its basic structure, *Le Testament* recalls more of *Le Sang d'un Poète* than *Orphée*, for the latter of these two films, with regard to its dialogue and fundamental communicative form, remains more of a narrative story, whereas the former

---

58. Some, as in the case of Francis Steegmuller's *Cocteau: A Biography*, curtly dismiss this film as "the mawkish *Testament d'Orphée*, a regrettable item in his film legacy." Others, as in Frederick Brown's *An Impersonation of Angels*, state simply that Cocteau did, in fact, film *Le Testament* and then they proceed to grossly underinterpret it with two or three vague and generalized sentences. There seem to be only a handful of authors who have, to any extent at all, attempted to comment in detail upon *Le Testament*. Elizabeth Sprigge and Jean-Jacques Kihm's *Jean Cocteau: The Man and the Mirror* and René Gilson's *Jean Cocteau* must be classified among these special few as well as, to a limited extent, Wallace Fowlie's *Jean Cocteau*. The most comprehensive and intriguing studies, however, seem to come in the form of three film reviews: the first, done by Roger Manvell, can be found in *Films and Filming*, 6 (July 1960) :24; another by Derek Prouse, is located in the film journal of *Sight and Sound*, 29 (Winter 1950–60) :18–19; and the last, by George Amberg, can be found in *Film Comment* 7, no. 4 (Winter 1971–72) :28–27. Without unduly "judging" *Le Testament* as a good or bad film, these three reviews offer exceptionally good coverage of what the film *is* and, in addition, offer numerous ideas as to possible interpretive keys with which to unravel Cocteau's vocabulary and imagery. Each clearly understands the previously discussed necessity of not trying to employ the standards of film-narrative for the clarification and judgment of film-poetry and, in that light, their respective reviews rank among the only viable guideposts for viewing *Le Testament d'Orphée*. As in the case of *Le Sang d'un Poète* and *Orphée*, there are several excellent studies in French that, at present, remain untranslated but which reveal to the "uninitiated" viewer of Cocteau a host of significant and instructive aids for familiarizing one with Cocteau's very personal cinematic vocabulary (*see* bibliography).

59. Pillandin.

reflects throughout the composite attributes of a true film-poem as defined within the first sections of this study.

For the purposes of clarification and interpretation, *Le Testament d'Orphée* may be broken down into roughly fourteen or fifteen "scenes" beginning with the opening sequence of the poet and the professor and ending with the poet's final death at the roadside. It must be understood, however, that these categorical divisions remain strictly arbitrary and that Cocteau, in designing the film, made no formal episodic separations as he had done in *Le Sang d'un Poète*. Such a breakdown seems mandatory, however, for two reasons. First, due to the massive quantities of thematic material present within this film, covering the complete gamut of Cocteau's life, works, and ideas, it would be highly unfeasible to proceed with a detailed interpretation from the standpoint of individual themes. And, second, a breakdown of *Le Testament* into successive scenes would seem to facilitate a detailed exposé of the film as a whole—an accomplishment, as yet, quite rare for this particular work of art.

Le Testament d'Orphée begins, then, with a half-serious parody on relativity involving the poet who is lost in space-time and seeks to escape his predicament by utilizing the services of a certain professor of science. The poet appears and disappears at various portions of the professor's life until, at last, he stops at the intended point of time. Having visited momentarily the professor's dying moments and having taken from the perished man's hands a small box, the poet then introduces himself to the now middle-aged man of science and presents to him this box containing a number of bullets. These bullets are very special for they can travel faster than light, and the poet realizes that they remain his only hope for terminating his endless wandering in space-time. The poet asks the professor to shoot him with one of these bullets and the professor kindly obliges. The poet falls to the ground and immediately bounces back to his feet, now in modern dress instead of the eighteenth-century attire he had previously been wearing. The poet, then appears to sleepwalk to the door of the laboratory and, thanking the professor, walks gently into the night, moving as if in slow motion.

This opening passage of *Le Testament*, where the poet is seemingly lost in a space-time continuum, reflects Cocteau's philosophic fascination with the concepts of relativity and their application to his own poetic beliefs regarding the relationship of the poet to the adjacent realities of the present and the beyond. It has been said that

Killed by a bullet traveling faster than light, the poet is reborn into the modern era. (COURTESY OF CONTEMPORARY FILMS/MC GRAW-HILL.)

Cocteau was inspired to include this scene as merely a parody of many of the young "nouvelle-vague" filmmakers of modern French cinema (Truffaut, Godard, and others) and their innovative efforts in creating "time-less" cinematic works. However, Cocteau's case seems quite a bit more profound and his motives much less eclectic than this view would seem to give him credit for. First of all, one has but to consider *Le Sang d'un Poète* of nearly thirty years prior to witness Cocteau's portrayal of a "time-less" film, symbolized in the form of a crumbling factory chimney at the debut and the conclusion of the film. Second, Cocteau's interest in the concepts of space and time seem to literally predate most of the contemporary cinematic vogues, for it was in the late 1940s that Cocteau wrote:

> Centuries have been necessary for man to get clear about the certainty that space and time are functions one of the other. . . . Time and space together form so elastic and so outrageous an amalgam that man is constantly finding himself faced with so little proofs that he really tends to get lost in it all. . . .

Time and space are but one, and it is only our laws which separate them. . . .[60]

Furthermore, Cocteau's extremely prevalent use of such terms as
quantum and *atoms* throughout his later essays suggests that his interest
in the relationship of time and space to man originated with the very
birth of the atomic age and Einstein's theories. Cocteau's concern
with this field, then, seems quite sincere and not the result of a mere
desire to imitate the techniques of the youthful cinéastes of his time.

One finds many other noteworthy ideas within this first scene as
well, aside from Cocteau's playful tamperings with space and time.
Consider, for instance, the poet's admonition to the professor who
wishes to "understand":

Professor, you must be the only person in the world capable of
not trying to understand and also understanding what is not understandable. . . .[61]

That is to say, men of science should be the first to realize that there
are realms of truth that they can not penetrate using the usual methods of deductive empiricism. And, due to this realization, they are
ironically closer to understanding than anyone else. "Don't ask me
why," Cocteau seems again to be stating. Persisting in his questions,
the professor asks again for an explanation, however, and the poet replies
simply: "Poets know quite a few . . . awesome things."[62] To which the
professor seems to concede, saying: "I sometimes think they know
far more than we do."[63] Hence, the opening scene seems to recount the
confrontation between the man of science and the man of poetry, the
latter needing the former to help him escape from his "half-existence"
bordering two worlds, yet, all the while, seeming to understand the
nature of the problem more than the man whom he asks for as-
sistance. Science, Cocteau seems to be saying, can not bridge the gap
to form a contact with the beyond—this function is reserved for the
poet and his creations.

To fulfill the poet's request, the professor "kills" him with a bullet
that travels faster than light (again, a reference to quantum theory
and Einstein's postulates). "Relatively" speaking, the poet "dies,"
and is reborn as a member of the professor's world—at least, for a

60. Cocteau, *The Hand of a Stranger*, pp. 58–59.
61. Cocteau, *Two Screenplays*, p. 89.
62. Cocteau, *Two Screenplays*, p. 89.
63. Ibid.

Cégeste (Edouard Dermit) is reincarnated from the sea, bringing to the poet a hibiscus flower. (COURTESY OF CONTEMPORARY FILMS/MC-GRAW-HILL.)

while. The poet's "death" in this opening scene recalls, once again, Cocteau's favorite theme of his essential "Orphic identity" and the necessity for a true poet to die and be reborn many times to achieve his ends. This particular "death" seems reminiscent of the poet's "transit": the poet's leaving of this world to join his "inner angel" or, perhaps more directly applicable, his return from the beyond to reside once more in the reality of the normal world in which he must create and be accordingly judged. Such deaths and rebirths on the part of the poet seem to constitute one of the predominant "messages" of *Le Testament d'Orphée,* and it is through this light of Orphic identity that many succeeding portions of this film may be respectively clarified.

Proceeding down a deserted road, the poet then meets a man-horse: a young man with his entire head covered by the mask of a horse and a horse's tail swaying behind him. The poet follows the man-horse to a gypsy camp surrounding a brightly burning campfire. From the flames of the fire a photo of Cégeste, a character from *Orphée,* slowly materializes and jumps to the hand of one of the gypsy women. The woman tears up the photo and hands it to the poet. The poet, holding the pieces of the shredded photo in his hand retreats from the gypsy camp and walks down a narrow path to the sea. He hurls the remnants of the photo into the breaking surf and watches as Cégeste, in person, flies up from the water and lands on the shore next to him. Cégeste then presents to the poet a large, red hibiscus flower, explaining to him that, as an expert in phoenixology, it is his job to bring the flower back to life. The poet questions Cégeste as to his meaning, but Cégeste admonishes him for trying too hard to understand and leads him into the night.

In this second major scene, the man-horse stands as an image very familiar to those "initiates" who have read a number of Cocteau's many works and recall the man-horse of Cocteau's play *Orphée* (later replaced by the Rolls-Royce of the film version). In both versions of *Orphée,* as now in *Le Testament d'Orphée,* the role played by the man-horse (or Rolls-Royce) seems to be rather ominous and a bearer of ill tidings to the ever-suffering poet. It is usually the man-horse, in all three of these works, who acts as the bait in an enigmatic and inevitably "fatal" trap; the poet allows himself to fall into this trap and, through one means or another, is forced to undergo terrible tribulations as a result. Eva Kushner observes that the man-horse is Cocteau's "dada."[64] Translated, "dada" has two very relevant definitions: a hobby or favorite preoccupation and a child's term designating a horse. Thus, particularly in its use within the two versions of *Orphée,* the man-horse seems a very appropriate entity to express the poet's preoccupation with his craft. But, further, "Dada" also is the name of a rather nihilistic avant-garde literary movement in Paris immediately following World War II (the forerunner of what was to later become Surrealism). In the light of this consideration, therefore, Cocteau's strange man-horse would seem to epitomize the poet's temptation to break with his own predetermined poetic identity and follow a more convenient path toward artistic greatness. From this point of view, the man-horse would seem to represent not only an entire realm of poetic "philosophy of revolt and destruction" as practiced by the avant-garde of Cocteau's time, but also these very rivals themselves and their attempts to entrap him and sway him from his assigned duties as a poet of the beyond. Such a temptation recalls, once again,

64. Eva Kushner, *Le Mythe d'Orphée dans la Littérature Française Contemporaine* (Paris: A. G. Nizet Publishers, 1961) , p. 183.

Christ in the Garden of Gethsemane and it would not seem too surprising if Cocteau intended this parallel.

The poet is put on trial before the tribunal, composed of personages from his film Orphée *(François Perier and Maria Césares).* (COURTESY OF CONTEMPORARY FILMS/MC GRAW-HILL.)

This sinister man-horse, then, leads the poet to the camp of the Gitans, a tribe of gypsies, where the poet is given a shredded photo of Cégeste, newly reincarnated from the flames of the campfire. Cocteau's fascination with gypsies proceeds, it seems, from a characteristic that they seem to share in common with many other items of Cocteau's poetic and personal vocabulary, for example, mirrors, opium, blood, statues, angels, et al. This attribute stems from the capacity of these particular items to reveal the poet to himself, to allow the poet, via an intermediary, to identify his true essence. Thus, Cocteau's interest in gypsies seems quite understandable, for these individuals are well known as fortune-tellers, tarot readers, and prophets of things to come. It could be well argued that, due to their common proximity to the beyond, Cocteau felt a significant kinship to gypsy-folk, much in the same way that he seemed to feel when watching acrobats perform in the circus. In any event, it is through gypsy magic that Cégeste's photograph materializes in the fire and, signifying perhaps Cégeste's previous "death" in *Orphée*, a gypsy woman tears up the picture and hands the remains to the man responsible for that death. The poet takes the photo, casts it into the sea, and witnesses the rebirth of Cégeste into the world of the living. Once more, it is the poet who *causes* the cycle to turn as a veteran expert in phoenixology, as Cégeste later asserts.

Returning from the "Zone," Cégeste presents the poet with a dead hibiscus flower. It is the poet's duty to bring this flower to life. The hibiscus flower seems to play an extremely important role in *Le Testament d'Orphée* and, as Cocteau states during the filming of *Le Testament,* a role that parallels that of himself: one of eternal death and resurrection. In fact, Cocteau had intended to subtitle his film *La Resurrection d'une Fleur* instead of *Ne Me Demandez Pas Pourquoi* (Don't Ask Me Why), but changed his mind and decided to utilize the latter as his answer to those who would "prefer to understand than to feel." The reasons why Cocteau chose the hibiscus, of all flowers, to play such an important part in his film are clarified by the author himself in quite simple terms:

> I chose the hibiscus flower simply because there are a lot of them in the garden here at Santo-Sospir. It's a magnificent flower, dark red with a vigorous pistil. A very strange flower, very disturbing, much less pretentious than the orchid.[65]

For whatever reason Cocteau originally chose the hibiscus, its role in *Le Testament* seems clear. The hibiscus flower seems to represent the poet's *artistic creation,* the concrete representation of his visions of the beyond. But, as it was in the film, the poet must give "life" to this survivor of another world and present it to humanity in the form of a "gift." Thus, Cégeste leads the poet away; this time to bring about a rebirth of a heretofore "dead" portion of his own self; to express in "living" form what is deep within him and, from the viewpoint of humanity, accordingly considered nonexistent. The concluding moments of this entire scene, therefore, suggest the aftermath of the poet's initial inspiration, before he actively attempts an acceptable "living" portrayal of this inspiration for his awaiting public.

Cégeste then leads the poet toward the lighthouse further down the coast. It is now dusk. On their way to a neighboring greenhouse, Cégeste and the poet pass by a young girl standing before Cocteau's

---

65. Pillaudin, p. 104.

Judith and Holofernes tapestry and she is answering various quizlike questions posed to her by a radio commentator. Finally entering the greenhouse, where one sees an empty flowerpot and an easel, Cégeste orders the poet to resurrect the dead flower, saying:

> Turn your night into day. Then we'll see who is giving the orders and who is carrying them out.[66]

The professor is summoned as a witness for the defense. (COURTESY OF CONTEMPORARY FILMS/MC GRAW-HILL.)

The poet then gathers up his brushes, approaches the easel, and tries to paint. However, the sheet repeatedly ripples, flies off, and reveals the large paintings of Cocteau's *Oedipus and his Daughter* and *Head of Orpheus*. A voice comments:

> Of course, works of art create themselves, and dream of killing both father and mother. Of course, they exist before the artist discovers them. But it's always "Orpheus," always "Oedipus."[67]

66. Cocteau, *Two Screenplays*, p. 98.
67. Ibid.

And Cégeste adds, from behind a skull mask that he has put over his face:

> Don't try anymore; a painter always paints his own portrait. You'll never succeed in painting that flower.[68]

The poet, furious, then grabs the hibiscus and tears it apart. Cégeste once again admonishes him, puts the remnants of the flower in the flowerpot and both Cégeste and the poet leave the greenhouse.

Cocteau's inclusion of this particular scene in *Le Testament* seems motivated by his desire to include as many of his artistic works in the film as possible, to fully portray his poetry, novels, paintings, and murals together, as if on display, one beside the other. It should be pointed out, however, that the tapestry of *Judith and Holofernes* was originally scheduled to be a part of a documentary film highlighting Cocteau's nonliterary artistic achievements, including such works as his mural in the Chapel of Villefranche and others. This idea was never acted upon, however, for Cocteau decided to create, instead, *Le Testament d'Orphée*. Not surprisingly, then, Cocteau included this tapestry in his autobiographical film and accomplished the same ends through entirely different means. Whatever the case, there are two noteworthy portions of this scene that seem to merit elaboration.

First, as the camera zooms in for a close-up of the tapestry itself, the commentator explains the history of its subject matter:

> Judith has just cut off the head of Nebuchadnezzar's captain, Holofernes. . . . Judith is no longer a woman . . . from now on she is the sarcophagus that contains her own legend. . . .[69]

As a "sarcophagus that contains her own legend," Judith seems to reflect very well the condition of her creator, Cocteau. For, as the preceding sections pointed out, Cocteau is preoccupied with the fact that his own identity, as a poet and as a man, was becoming "mythicized" within the minds of contemporary society. He was, at the age of sixty, already a walking incarnation of his own notorious and famed legend. It seems rather significant, then, in this personal light, that Cocteau would speak of the tapestry of *Judith and Holofernes* as a depiction of the moment when Judith reached her lasting immortality,

---

68. Ibid., p. 99.
69. Cocteau, *Two Screenplays*, p. 96.

particularly when compared to the subject matter of the entire film in which this scene is cast—that is, a delineation of the successive steps toward the immortality of Jean Cocteau himself!

Second, the young girl's dialogue reveals a humorous play on words between "violon dingue" and "violon d'Ingres," when referring to Cocteau's pastimes. The term *violon d'Ingres* translates as a pet hobby at which one excels: a very appropriate description of the talents that brought Cocteau to create the tapestry of *Judith and Holofernes*. However, "violon dingue" is a bit more difficult to translate and seems to consist of two slang terms juxtaposed. A "violon" is a very idiomatic French expression referring to jail—much like "hoosegow" in American slang. A "dingue," is, on the other hand, modern French slang describing someone or something who is very much out of the ordinary or someone who is slightly demented. If such are the meanings intended by Cocteau, this latter term would suggest the quasi-comical ravings of an eccentric prisoner—also, perhaps, applicable to Cocteau's case and his resulting tapestry.

A lady (Mme. Alec Weisweiller), dressed in the manner of a young Sarah Bernhardt, has mistaken her era. (COURTESY OF CONTEMPORARY FILMS/MC GRAW-HILL.)

Hence, this scene of Judith and Holofernes once more illustrates two elements of Cocteau's essential Orphic identity: his immortality through his works and his sensitivity to public ridicule for being someone who is "different." But what looms as perhaps Cocteau's most obvious reason for including this very "discontinuous" scene into *Le Testament* was his simple desire to portray as many of his own artistic creations as possible within his final cinematic epitaph and tribute to his poetic life.

The portion of this scene where Cégeste and the poet are in the greenhouse trying to revive the hibiscus, offers many interesting and rather significant insights into the relationship of the poet to his creation. Cégeste challenges the poet to "turn his night into day"; that is to say, the poet must materialize the visions of his "night," his inner "beyond," into an acceptable art form for all to see and appreciate. As the poet attempts to paint a picture of the flower, however, the brush strokes guide themselves and reveal the portraits of Oedipus and Orpheus. Cégeste aptly observes, as Cocteau's mouthpiece, that works of art create themselves and demand the death of "both father and mother." This statement by Cégeste echoes one of the main tenets of Cocteau's poetic philosophy: the poet is one who is "possessed," that his creations are really not his at all but originate from the beyond, and that they use him only as a tool to facilitate their own worldly manifestation. Such works then "turn" on their author, for coexistence between creator and creation results in the confusion of their identities and neither can be fully appreciated in the company of the other. This necessary "death" of the artist with regard to his works constitutes one of the many "Orphic" deaths that the true poet must endure to achieve immortality. Such figurative deaths are represented by the portraits of Oedipus (who was truly the cause of his parents' deaths) and Orpheus (who, like the artist, underwent similar successive deaths in the name of poetry).

The poet tries one final time to accurately paint the hibiscus but succeeds only in creating a portrait of himself. Cégeste reminds the poet that true representation is impossible, and that the artist will only find a better picture of himself as the results of his efforts to portray his visions. Such a statement on Cégeste's part reflects to a large degree Cocteau's three autobiographical films of *Le Sang d'un Poète, Orphée,* and *Le Testament d'Orphée* taken up in this study. Each, trying to effectively and objectively portray the poet's "night" and his creative process, consummates in a personalized and very self-revealing portrait of the artist's identity rather than the identity of his "night."

The poet, then, in a fit of frustrated anger, "kills" his yet-to-be-born flower, and Cégeste, echoing perhaps what the poet himself feels inside, tells him that he should be ashamed of himself; shame for having momentarily lost faith in his "angel," shame for believing that his own role is anything but that of a "humble servant," shame for trying to nullify that inspiration upon which his own life finds its meaning.

The poet and Cégeste then arrive at a patio decorated with mosaics done by Cocteau. Cégeste then puts the flower and flowerpot on a table and the poet, now dressed in an Oxford gown and mortarboard, proceeds to pull out what is left of the hibiscus and brings it back to life. Mending the torn petals one by one, the poet finishes by replacing the pistil. Cégeste then proposes that the poet carry the re-created flower to Pallas Athena and offer it as a gift to the goddess. The poet refuses, but when Cégeste reminds him that it was he who had left Cégeste in the underworld, in Cocteau's film *Orphée*, the poet decides to obey. They then disappear into the villa.

The "Idol of Fame" digests autographs and produces instant celebrity.
(COURTESY OF CONTEMPORARY FILMS/MC GRAW-HILL.)

Cocteau indicates, via this particular scene, that the poet's inspiration has finally been tempered, via many trials and tribulations, into an acceptable "living" flower. This rebirth of the hibiscus is accomplished through the magic arts of the poet—reassembling each individual petal laboriously until the entire flower springs wondrously to life. The poet's Oxford garb is also quite relevant to his task. Cégeste addresses the poet as "Docteur," in deference to his academic apparel, but this title seems all the more significant when considering the "medical" nature of the poet's efforts in transforming the dead to the living. Further, the poet's Oxford dress reflects Cocteau's strict demands for technical discipline when trying to make the unreal real and the dead alive. It is primarily due to Cocteau's sense of classic discipline when portraying his visions that one can not classify him as an entirely avant-garde literary figure, and one must concede that his works have a definitely "traditional" flavor at times. Such associations are very closely connected and quickly come to mind when watching the traditionally academic-uniformed poet performing his miracle of bringing his flower to life. But, as prior sections of this study have pointed out, the poet's task is not complete until his work of art has been repeatedly judged and received, for good or ill, by its public. Thus, Cégeste informs the poet of the necessity of bringing the hibiscus before Minerva and, after some hesitation, the poet reluctantly obeys.

The poet is then led into a room reminiscent of the tribunal chamber of the film *Orphée*. Seated as judges one recognizes at once the familiar Princesse and Heurtebise. The poet is severely interrogated and must answer to two crimes: first, the crime of innocence and, secondly, the crime of desiring to penetrate a world that is not his. The professor who had "killed" the poet is summoned as a witness from his deep sleep and, after answering several questions, is returned to his slumber. The verdict is nearly at hand when the poet is asked for his defense. He replies:

> I would like to say that if I deserve punishment, I can not imagine any more painful one than being forced to live between two worlds, or to use your own words, between two realms. . . . I'd give anything to be able to walk on solid ground again, and, not to be lost in the shadows of a strange universe.[70]

Having heard the evidence, the "court" condemns the poet to a "life sentence," and promptly adjourns. Speaking with Heurtebise following the trial, the poet learns of the punishment accorded to the Princesse and Heurtebise at the conclusion of *Orphée*: to pay for their crimes, they had been condemned to judging others forever. The Princesse

---

70. Cocteau, *Two Screenplays*, p. 114.

and Heurtebise disappear and Cégeste once more leads the poet away.

Within this particular scene Cocteau interjects (via the poet) many of his own beliefs regarding the nature of a poet and the poet's craft. When asked the motivation for his "crimes," the poet replies to the judges:

> Probably because I am tired of the world I live in. . . . Also because of that disobedience with which audacity defies the rules, and that spirit of creation which is the highest form of the spirit of contradiction—pertaining to human beings.[71]

Thus, Cocteau weaves into his response to his critics a proclamation of defiance and a tribute to artists' disobedience and contradiction. Such a reply recalls Cocteau's extensive use of what he liked to term *truthful lies* and his many other seemingly contradictory statements that had, throughout his life, been brought repeatedly to his attention by an exasperated public.

When asked to define his conception of "film," the poet-Cocteau replies:

> A film is a petrifying source of thought. A film revives dead acts—a film allows one to give a semblance of reality to unreality.[72]

In so saying, Cocteau reveals once again his preference for the art form of the film as the ultimate vehicle for poetic communication. Through film one may "revive dead acts": that is to say, the poet may bring about a rebirth of his original inspirations dictated to him from the beyond and portray them in a befitting manner available through no other art form. Further, Cocteau seems to be once more playing with words, for this film itself, *Le Testament d'Orphée*, stands as a composite rebirth of the many "dead acts" of Cocteau's life and artistic endeavors. Due to the cinema's innate capacity for creating believability, and its ability to manipulate time and space, film is, for Cocteau, the perfect medium in making the unreal real and having such a portrayal remain credible to a questioning public.

When asked to define a "poet," the poet replies:

> The poet, by composing poems, uses a language that is neither dead nor living, that few people speak and few people understand.[73]

---

71. Cocteau, *Two Screenplays*, p. 103.
72. Ibid., p. 104.
73. Cocteau, *Two Screenplays*, p. 105.

The court usher (Yul Brynner) delays the poet's entrance into Minerva's chambers. (COURTESY OF CONTEMPORARY FILMS/MC GRAW-HILL.)

Once again Cocteau stresses the poet's role as being one who, through a magical use of language, bridges the gap between the living and the dead, that is, between man and the beyond. Due to the oracular and necessarily complex nature of such a language, Cocteau asserts that few people speak or even understand it. Such a practice is the prerogative and the duty of poets alone. Cocteau implies, as well, that the poet is inevitably one who is grossly misunderstood and misinterpreted because of an inherent "language barrier" between himself and his public. They seek to "understand" via rational means whereas the poet seeks to communicate via means that defy the dictates of reason.

When asked for the origin of this "language which is neither living nor dead," the poet answers: "We are the servants of an unknown force that lives within us, manipulates us, and dictates this language to us."[74] In one brief and concise sentence, Cocteau defines the role of the poet: he is one who is forever "possessed" and who is at the orders of his "night." As previously pointed out elsewhere, Cocteau's

74. Ibid., p. 107.

conception of the poet's inspiration is built upon the fact that the poet is, by nature, an oracle and transmits messages from the beyond, in the manner of a servant who would faithfully carry out his master's orders. Cocteau's entire poetic philosophy is constructed with this central theme as a starting point, and it is not at all surprising to find Cocteau's elaboration of this theme within the plot of *Le Testament d'Orphée.*

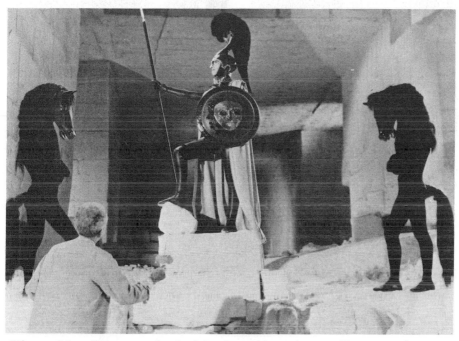

The goddess Minerva, flanked by her aides, gives audience to the poet. (COURTESY OF CONTEMPORARY FILMS/MC GRAW-HILL.)

Following this series of philosophic questions directed at the poet by the tribunal, the Princesse interviews the professor whom she has summoned from his sleep. Learning of the poet's "death" and "rebirth" into his present identity via the bullets that traveled faster than light, the Princesse then dismisses the professor and turns her attention once more to the accused. She addresses the poet saying:

I am aware that the detours on your road are a sort of labyrinth— quite different from ours, although they intermingle—and that although you were able to find the only person who could correct your mistakes and your disobedience of terrestrial laws, this was

not because of absentmindedness on the part of the unknown, but
because of a kind of supreme indulgence that you abuse, dear
sir. . . .[75]

Rather nebulous at the outset of the trial, the poet's crimes now become clear. The poet stands accused as one who not only transgresses
the laws of man (due to the very fact that he is a poet), but also, as a
result of his encounter with the professor, he has transgressed the laws
of the beyond. He has acquiesced to the temptation of forsaking his
poetic identity and becoming a "normal" human being. He has be-
trayed his duty as a messenger between the two worlds, desiring the
security of anonymity and the peace of irresponsibility. Such an act
resembles the "mauvaise foi" exhibited by the poet of the film *Le Sang
d'un Poète* when he demolished the statue, and of the film *Orphée*
when Orphée allowed himself to copy dictated messages sent via the
radio of the Rolls-Royce instead of searching his own soul for inspiration. The presence of such episodes in all three of these intensely autobiographical films suggests that Cocteau is not a poet without self-
doubt and an occasional yearning for an identity not associated with
that of a poet. Parallel to the temptations of Christ in the Garden of
Gethsemane, Cocteau is a figure who is tempted by the desire for personal comfort and plagued by the realization of his own destiny. The
poet elaborates Cocteau's case: "I'd give anything to be able to walk
on solid ground again, and not to be lost in the shadows of a strange
universe. . . ."[76] But, unlike Christ, Cocteau tries again and again to
defy his destiny as a poet and shed the chains that bind him to his interior "angel." However, as every true poet must come to realize, Cocteau's fate is inexorable and unmoved by the mere personal desires of
man. Try as he will to deny his own identity, the beyond will inevitably reclaim his services as its ambassador to humanity. And, as punishment for his temporary loss of faith, the Princesse condemns the
poet-Cocteau, saying: "The board of inquiry condemns you to the life
sentence."[77] That is to say, the poet-Cocteau shall *never*, throughout
his long life, be permitted to escape from what he knows to be his own
identity as a poet. The poet-Cocteau shall *always* continue to stand
with one foot in life and the other in death as an oracle, an intermediary, an acrobat perched precariously upon the thin wire separating
the present and the hereafter. The poet-Cocteau is thus forever locked

75. Cocteau, *Two Screenplays*, p. 112.
76. Cocteau, *Two Screenplays*, p. 114.
77. Ibid.

to his own "Orphic cycle" of poetic creation and public scrutiny and shall continue to suffer the repeated deaths and rebirths necessary to accomplish the demands of his "night."

The poet is impaled by Minerva's spear. (COURTESY OF CONTEMPORARY FILMS/MC GRAW-HILL.)

After reaching their verdict, the tribunal fades from view. Yet Heurtebise remains behind a moment and speaks to the poet. The poet learns that Heurtebise and the Princesse are now forced to be judges; that was the punishment accorded to them at the close of *Orphée*. The poet shudders at the thought. This final portion of the scene seems rather significant if one but considers the fame and worldwide acclaim of Cocteau's film *Orphée* as compared to the relatively unseen and unacknowledged majority of his other cinematic works. As such, *Orphée* would undoubtedly become for Cocteau's cinema critics an evaluative standard to "judge" the quality of these other lesser known film works, as well as Cocteau himself as their creator. Cocteau seemed to recognize this eventuality and, as a perfect rejoinder to answer these critics' many questions as to the undefined outcome of the Princesse and Heurtebise in *Orpheé*, he chose to typecast these characters as "judges," appraising their author's worth as well as his other artistic creations.

And, as a final irony, Cocteau chose to insert this particular scene into the one film that he believed would be the most apt to be compared to and judged by his original *Orphée*, *Le Testament d'Orphée*!

Traversing a garden in front of the villa, Cégeste and the poet then find themselves in the company of a lady dressed "in the manner of a young Sarah Bernhardt," who carries a Japanese parasol and is reading a paperback murder-mystery. She calls to her butler and asks him the outcome of the story. Learning of his ignorance, she replies a bit perturbed:

> It's incredible. Are you going to force me to read an entire book that won't appear for another seventy years?[78]

Finally catching sight of the poet and Cégeste, the lady asks her butler if he knows their identity. Once again the butler can not answer, for he can not see the two intruders. The lady then seems truly upset and, commenting upon the "strangeness of the times," she blows a small whistle and calls to her two young swimmers who don the garb of Anubis—one wearing a mask as the head and the other comprising the tail—and who precede their mistress into the house. The poet asks Cégeste, "Who is she?" And Cégeste, annoyed, answers:

> Don't be silly. That's a confused lady who is in the wrong era. You should be the first to know that these things can happen.[79]

Cocteau's inclusion of this particular scene remains a mystery, though it has been said that the doglike antics of the two swimmers were originally suggested by Picasso and his studio decors from the stageplay *Parade* (1917), in which he participated along with Cocteau and Eric Satie.[80] Whatever the case, the lady of the scene seems to closely parallel the poet's capacity for time-travel and reveals very aptly the resulting confusion of such time alterations that plagued the poet at the debut of *Le Testament*. In reference to this scene, Cocteau has stated: "It's the intemporal theme of mixing the real and the unreal, space and time."[81] But he refuses to clarify his intent beyond this point. Whether or not the intention was there, Cocteau seems to characterize in this "lost" woman all of those "monstres sacrés" of his early literary career who had a great and lasting effect upon him; the turn-of-the-century

---

78. Cocteau. *Two Screenplays*, p. 116.
79. Ibid., p. 118.
80. Cf., Pillaudin, p. 114.
81. Pillaudin, p. 110.

The horse-men remove the spear from the poet's body and carry him to his deathbed. (COURTESY OF CONTEMPORARY FILMS/MC GRAW-HILL.)

"greats" who, like himself, were gifted with the poetic capacity of forcing time to remain immobile and, accordingly, rendering themselves chronologically immortal. Cocteau once made allusion to the fact that all great artists must live beyond the means of their time. Such being the case, it would seem very appropriate that this elegant lady, living beyond her own age, would epitomize such great artists in Cocteau's early life as Sarah Bernhardt, Colette, Gertrude Stein, a cabaret singer named Mistinguett, the Comtesse Anna de Noailles, Misia Sert, Valentine Hugo, CoCo Chanel, and a host of other personalities who were to help mold the young, precocious Cocteau into the serious poet of his later years.

As the poet and Cégeste continue on their way they catch sight of a yacht called *Orphée II,* which is sailing out to sea. The poet asks if the woman seen on board is the goddess. Cégeste replies:

No, that's Iseult. She is aboard all the ships in the world. She is looking for Tristram.[82]

---

82. Cocteau, *Two Screenplays,* p. 120.

This brief scene recalls Cocteau's film of the same mythic origin entitled *L'Eternel Retour*. The irony of the scene, however, lies in the fact that Iseult is sailing upon a vessel named *Orphée II*, and is searching for her lost love, much in the same manner as Cocteau seems to be searching for his mythic identity via a reincarnation of the personage of Orpheus in his own works. The fact that sailboat in French is "bateau à voile" and that "voile" also signifies a veil undoubtedly led Cocteau to theorize of this scene:

> Since I detest the style of phantoms, I see a real woman surrounded by sails [veils].[83]

Thus, in addition to its more profound significances, the scene of Iseult aboard the *Orphée II* affords to Cocteau another opportunity to illustrate his artistic discipline necessary for making the imagery very real, for giving a myth of the past a life in the present.

Cégeste then leads the poet down a narrow alleyway called *Rue Obscure* where the poet passes his double who ignores him and continues by without a word. The poet, astounded by his other self, asks why he did not greet them. Cégeste merely suggests that the double has been kicked around and insulted too much in the place of the poet. The poet says that he will kill the double, but Cégeste cautions him against it, for the poet's immortality would be in vain if he could never find anyone else who would allow himself to be killed in the poet's place.

According to an addition made in the original scenario, Cocteau termed this particular scene one of the *backbones* of *Le Testament*. It is, appropriately enough, on Obscure Street that Cocteau meets face to face with himself—or, rather, the self that could be termed his *social identity*: the publicized Cocteau created by years of notoriety, scandal, and legend. This twin represents the "visible" Cocteau, whereas the poet incarnates the Cocteau that the public does not see, the "invisible" poet, working behind the scenes and creating immortal works of art with his life's blood. The double passes by the poet in silence and Cégeste points out that the double has no reason to like the poet, for he has been "insulted and kicked around enough instead of you." But Cégeste also cautions the poet not to kill the double, for the poet would be hard pressed, immortal though he may be, to find another to take the double's place and be repeatedly killed. Such a desire on the poet's part to "kill" his double seems to reflect Cocteau's

---

83. Pillaudin, p. 150.

A circle of the poet's closest friends (including Pablo Picasso) watch him "die." (COURTESY OF CONTEMPORARY FILMS/MC GRAW-HILL.)

personal inclination to withdraw his own protective "cloak of invisibility" in the face of his public and, thus, destroy his oftentimes salutary, dichotomized identity as a poet and as a man. But, as Cégeste so aptly observes, Cocteau would then be left unprotected, exposed and, in the widest sense possible, in danger of "death" at the hands of those who think they know him. Thus, to be left in peace, Cocteau decides to leave intact his split identity of his "visible" versus "invisible" selves. But what seems strangely meaningful, as regards Cocteau's identity preoccupation and the Orphic nature of his many selves, is one line of dialogue found near the conclusion of this scene. Cégeste admonishes the poet for asking too many questions and then concludes: "You spend your whole time trying to be, which prevents you from living."[84] This statement seems to very effectively capsulize Cocteau's entire identity fixation and, as Cocteau himself admits via his character of Cégeste, it is this very fixation that prevents the poet from truly living. Such a personal realization on Cocteau's part concerning his own na-

---

84. Cocteau, *Two Screenplays*, p. 122.

ture stands as one of the more remarkable portions of *Le Testament d'Orphée* and reveals Cocteau as an artist who, contrary to the beliefs of many of his critics, is very much aware of who he is, what he is, and how he is portraying himself via his works.

Entering the quarrylike setting of the temple of Minerva, Cégeste and the poet pass by two "intellectual lovers" who are simultaneously taking notes, and then come to a large hall in the midst of a quarrylike mass of ruins. Two young children come running down the blocks of stone and ask for autographs. They then take the autographs to a strange statuelike oracle in a long white robe and a head with several eyes and mouths. The children "feed" the autographs into the statue and, instantly, long ribbons of paper are produced from the idol's many mouths and float, fluttering in the air. Cégeste explains:

> It's a machine that will make anyone famous in a few minutes. Later, one has to try to be known. . . .[85]

"Pretend that you are crying, my friends, since poets only pretend they are dead." Whereupon the poet is reborn once more. (COURTESY OF CONTEMPORARY FILMS/MC GRAW-HILL.)

85. Cocteau, *Two Screenplays*, p. 123.

This first rather amusing image seems a parody à la Cocteau on the attributes of heterosexual love and how it may well be a process of the inquisitive mind rather than an instinctual gut reaction of the soul. Such a form of love contrasts highly with an artist's love for his creations; the latter can never be carried out through such "objective" observation and note taking. The second image is a bit more profound. The poet and Cégeste are suddenly besieged by two young children demanding autographs. The slips of paper are fed into an idol that spews forth poetry, novels, and other literary works of art. This "Idol of Fame," Cégeste explains, makes anyone an instant celebrity, but it is only much later that one becomes truly known. This scene, once again, reflects Cocteau's incessant preoccupation with his "public identity." Famed throughout the world because of his "legend," Cocteau feels that his "true" self and the "true" nature of his works have remained essentially unknown and "invisible" to the public eye. As mentioned earlier in this study, however, Cocteau feels that his position of being known yet unknown as a poet permits his being "discovered," which is the ideal of all artists.[86]

Approaching the "inner sanctum" where the goddess resides, Cégeste is forced to take his leave of the poet, who calls to him desperately. Alone now, the poet awaits. An usher, dressed in a tuxedo, tells him that, if he but waits a few minutes more, he will be permitted entrance to the chamber. The poet waits endlessly. Suddenly the usher ominously warns him: "Abandon hope all ye who enter here."[87]

Penetrating ever deeper into the abyss of the temple, Cégeste has taken his leave of the poet, who must now face the goddess Minerva alone with his re-created hibiscus. The fact that Cégeste abandons the poet at this point suggests perhaps that the artist's works must face public acceptance and/or rejection on their own merits, unencumbered by previous poetic endeavors or other outside influences. In any event, the poet is forced to wait endlessly for admittance to the chamber of Minerva. An usher announces that, if he would be kind enough to wait a bit longer, the goddess would deign to see him. The necessity of the waiting poet also finds its counterpart in Cocteau's poetic philosophy. Cocteau undoubtedly suggests via this scene that the artist must wait ceaselessly for his public to take notice of and receive his poetic works; but, further, this waiting period reflects

86. Cf., André Fraigneau, *Entretiens Autour du Cinematographie* (Paris: Editions André Bonne, 1961), pp. 58–59.
87. Cocteau, *Two Screenplays*, p. 123.

what Cocteau feels to be the characteristic pose of the works themselves with regard to their creator. As he explains:

> I have just said that Muses should be represented in attitudes of waiting. All Arts can and must wait. They often have to wait for the death of their makers before they are able to live.[88]

Thus, the poet's long period of waiting and expectation recalls not only the relationship of the artist to his public or the artist's creations to their public, but also that strange and unique bond linking the artist to his own works. As Cocteau pointed out repeatedly in his complex poetic philosophy, the poet's creation can live truly only after the figurative and/or literal "death" of its creator. Such a wait on the part of the artists' work, therefore, constitutes one portion of the poet's extensive Orphic identity. It is only through death that life can be reborn. And it is for such a death that the artist's works, and ultimately the artist himself, must await patiently.

Finally, the poet confronts, face to face, the goddess Minerva. She is perched high atop a pedestal, dressed in a black wetsuit, robe, and ornate helmet and flanked on both sides by two horse-men similar to the one that the poet encountered at the outset of his journey. The poet offers his flower to Minerva, but she turns away. Stammering, the poet backs away and turns to leave. Minerva brandishes her spear and throws. The spear sinks into the poet's back and protrudes from his chest. He falls to the ground murmuring, "How horrible . . . oh, how horrible. . . ." The horse-men descend, pull the spear from the poet's body, and carry him away to a circle of his "friends." The blood of the poet and the hibiscus flower on the ground turn red.

Cocteau portrays within this climactic scene *the poet's reception by his public* and the torment, the "death," that he and his works must undergo at the hands of an uncompromising and aloof host of critics. But what goddess is this who slays poets and shuns their hard-earned flowers of poetry? Cocteau explains that Minerva is the *Goddess of Reason*. Flanked, appropriately enough, by her ominous horse-men, this Goddess of Reason incarnated the hard-shelled logic and skepticism of the poet's public, to whom the poet's efforts seem incoherent and, thus, "unpoetic." Such an image of vengeful condemnation from the hand of reason applies exceptionally well to the entire evaluative predicament of the art form of film-poetry as contrasted to film-narrative with regard to their respective public appraisals. A film-poem,

---

88. Fraigneau, *Cocteau on the Film*, p. 13.

Leaving the temple, the poet passes the tragic figures of Oedipus and Antigone (Jean Marais and Brigitte Morissan). (COURTESY OF CON-TEMPORARY FILMS/MC GRAW-HILL.)

like the poet's flower, can not be judged simply according to the precepts of film-narrative; that is, according to its logical plot, its clearly cut image progressions, and its "entertainment" qualities. Confronted by such false evaluative criteria, conditioned within the public through traditionally accepted and standardized codes of meaning, the film-poem would invariably seem enigmatic, frustrating, and ill contrived. So it goes with the poet before his supreme judge, Minerva, and he is accordingly "killed" for his poetic audacity.

Sitting amid rubble, barbed wire, and a few of his onlooking friends, the poet then "dies"—his eyes are wide open and smoke curls from his mouth. But as the commentary suggests: "Pretend that you are crying, my friends, since poets only pretend they are dead."[89] And, instantly, the poet rises to his feet and walks from the hall as in a trance.

The poet's "death," and the mingling of his life's blood with the hibiscus flower, thus leads to his eventual resurrection. With the await-

89. Cocteau, *Two Screenplays*, p. 137.

The poet blindly passes the Sphinx. (COURTESY OF CONTEMPORARY FILMS/MC GRAW-HILL.)

ed "death" of its creator coming to pass, the artist's work may finally live and take his place on earth. It is through this Orphic progression that the poet is resurrected and achieves lasting immortality within men's minds. The poet's death is as symbolic a consummation of his life's work as that of Christ, and his eventual afterlife is as deeply embroidered within the fabric of myth as that of Orpheus. And it is through such a death and rebirth that Cocteau's Orphic cycle of artistic creation completes another turn. As the poet himself states, concerning his essential phoenixology in *Le Testament d'Orphée*:

> Dali invented a very lovely term: *phoenixology*. It is the science of dying many times in order to be reborn. The legend of the Phoenix desires that he die and be reborn endlessly. It's also the role of the poet. To suffer endlessly, to die a number of times to be reborn. The poet burns to become ashes. And, in their turn, the ashes change him into himself, thanks to this phenomenon of phoenixology.[90]

90. Pillaudin, p. 84.

Thus, the poet springs back to "life," complete with artificial eyes, and departs once more.

Leaving the "temple," the poet passes a Sphinx and the tragic figure of Oedipus, who is leaning on Antigone and whispering incomprehensible words. The poet sees nothing and continues walking down a deserted road toward the mountains. One hears:

COMMENTARY

> I awoke from this walking sleep on a road, and while I was wondering which way to go, I thought I heard the motorcyclists from my film *Orphée*. I knew what they were doing. I would have to undergo the same death as Cégeste.[91]

It, is, however, the police who approach the poet and ask for his identity papers. Producing the required documents, the poet watches the two policemen discuss the situation. But Cégeste immediately appears and beckons to the poet to follow him. The poet follows and, in a body configuration reminiscent of the crucifixion of Christ, he disappears into the roadside rocks. Cégeste explains: "After all, the earth is not your country,"[92] Meanwhile, the policemen have recognized the poet's name and, turning to ask for his autograph, are stunned to find that he is no longer there. The poet's identity card is dropped and materializes into the hibiscus flower as it touches the ground. A sports car full of young people passes by at great speed and the policemen turn to give chase. The flower flutters in the dust and is blown away as the sports car fades into the distance followed closely behind by the two policemen on motorcycles. Cocteau then signals the end of his film saying:

COMMENTARY And that's all. A joyful wave has spread across my farewell film. If it did not please you, I am sad, for I gave it all I could. . . .

My Star is a hisbiscus flower. . . .[93]

The entire film then concludes with the completion of a handdrawing of Orpheus, and a soap bubble that transforms into smoke, lettering the word *Fin*.

---

91. Cocteau, *Two Screenplays*, p. 143.
92. Ibid.
93. Ibid.

The police (reminiscent of the motorcyclists of Orphée) *stop the poet and question his identity.* (COURTESY OF CONTEMPORARY FILMS/MC-GRAW-HILL.)

In this final scene of *Le Testament*, the poet passes, without seeing them, the Sphinx and Oedipus of Thebes—those mythic legends that he had given life through his works and among whom he now walks as the incarnation of his own myth, the living myth of the immortal poet. Following his ironic confrontation with the police, who question his identity, the poet "dies" one final time, returning to his inspiring world of shadows from whence he came. He no longer has his artificial eyes and one must assume that this final death concerns not the mythicized poet but, rather, the poet who still lived as a man after the harrowing, though necessary, incident with the Goddess of Reason; for, as Cocteau would be the first to insist, a poet may live many identities simultaneously. In any event, Cégeste meaningfully observes as he leads the poet into the invisible world: "After all, the earth is not your country."[94] That is to say, in much the same manner as was declared by the tribunal, the poet may never permanently reside in the land

---

94. Cocteau, *Two Screenplays*, p. 143.

of the living but must endlessly oscillate between the two realms of the present and the beyond. Such is his duty as a poet, and it is only by means of such a shuttling back and forth through his Orphic cycle that his identity as a poet is determined. It is not insignificant that, at the point of the poet's disappearance among the rocks of the roadside, his body contorts into a configuration reminiscent of Christ's crucifixion upon the cross.

Thus, the cycle completes its full turn and the poet must, once again, begin his journey toward poetic creation outside of the limits of the normal world. One feels that the poet has been returned to the sources of his inspiration, and that the cycle of phoenixology, allowing him to bring about poetic creation, is once more underway beyond the scope of the screen. The poet's identity is now manifest in the hibiscus flower—a symbol, perhaps, of all that the poet leaves to humanity in the form of his life's art.

Cocteau then bids his farewell to his audience, calls attention to the hibiscus flower (as well he may!), and completes his sketch of the profile of Orpheus—one final and very appropriate double entendre as he concludes his own cinematic autoportrait.

Le Testament d'Orphée, then, stands as Jean Cocteau's final cinematic farewell to his public and, as such, attempts to reveal the poet's "famed yet unknown" poetic identity to those who have for so long failed to penetrate his "invisibility" as an artist and as a man. *Le Testament* appropriately concludes Cocteau's cinematic trio of autobiographical film-poems begun in 1932 with *Le Sang d'un Poète* and further elaborated in *Orphée* of 1950. As a self-proclaimed memorial to his life's works and to this "night" that determined his identity as a poet, *Le Testament* goes perhaps the furthest of these three films, and of any of Cocteau's works, in painting a succinct portrait of this now legendary French poet and filmmaker.

Conclusion

In conclusion, then, it seems evident that film-poetry, as manifest via the experimental cinema within the United States and other European films, has been largely ignored and, oftentimes, even condemned by the majority of the American movie-going public. Such a violent reaction to this particular genre of cinema seems essentially a product of a basic lack of understanding by the American viewer of what to expect through film-poetry and of how it differs from the more prevalent forms of film-narrative to which he has long grown accustomed. In order to familiarize the prospective viewer of film-poetry with the fundamental characteristics of this genre, it has been analyzed in contrast with the more easily recognizable forms of film-narrative and subsequently defined in terms of three criteria: purpose, structure, and audience interaction.

It has been shown that, whereas the prime purpose of film-narrative is to "entertain," film-poetry seeks to portray the artist's "inner vision" and, thus, communicate with the viewer on a deeper and more personal level of consciousness. Whereas the structure of film-narrative proceeds according to the traditional storytelling pattern of a logically constructed and linear plot development, film-poetry seeks to communicate primarily through visual suggestion and coordinates its imagery so as to create highly meaningful individual combinations that transcend their own literal interpretation and become archetypal representations of human "states of being." And, finally, whereas the viewer of film-narrative, desiring "entertainment," enters into a state of voluntary and passive anonymity, "losing" himself in his total identification with the drama-filled action on the screen, the viewer of film-poetry is constantly challenged, provoked, and forced to search within himself to discover meaning.

Hence, the attributes of film-poetry are seen to differ greatly from what the average, American film watcher has, through the years, grown acclimated to experiencing. And it is only after such an initiation to this opposing form of cinema that the public can better become able to broaden its heretofore constricted and narrow perspectives with regard to the appreciation of film as a viable and quite meaningful art form.

In the light of the foregoing discussion, therefore, a lengthy re-evaluation of one of the first experimenters with film-poetry, Jean Cocteau, was initiated. In order to attune the prospective viewer of Cocteau to the artist's own operative and symbolic vocabulary, an extensive investigation into Cocteau's poetic philosophy, artistic discipline, and public reception was attempted, and the discussion was completed with a look at two of the artist's most preferred themes, death and Orpheus.

With regard to Cocteau's poetic philosophy, it was learned that the artist's definition of "poetry" stands for an "artistic creation," regardless of genre of form and, accordingly, a "poet" is simply a "creator of art." Poetry itself, as Cocteau conceived of it, seems to be definable for him, as well, as a communicative "state of being"—a spiritual "way of seeing"—that, once effected through an art form, can permit man to rise above the everyday barriers of space and time and penetrate the "beyond." The poet, within this framework, is seen as the messenger of the "beyond," the inspired oracle, the mouthpiece. The poet's sole duty is to act as a communicator of the coded enigmas that originate from deep within himself but which are not his. The poet's "inspiration," then, is one of being "possessed" by what Cocteau chose to term as his *angel,* who resides deep within the poet's "inner night." Perhaps as a direct result of his repeated use of opium as a method of facilitating his communication with this "angel," Cocteau invariably turned to the theme of "death" when speaking of the poet's inspiration—this theme that, later in his life, became one of his most predominant artistic and spiritual fixations. Thus, the question of poetic inspiration for Jean Cocteau seems definable primarily via the metaphors of "death" and "angelism." Through the former, the poet arrives at a communication with the latter, and the poet's task of bridging the present and the hereafter is partially fulfilled.

As the section on reception illustrated, however, the poet must convey his inspiration to his public—his visions must take concrete form. And, as Cocteau was always quick to affirm, a rigorous sense of discipline is mandatory if one is to make the unreal real. Rather post-Romantic in his poetic ideology, Cocteau was very much a classicist in his theories of artistic portrayal. As his instruments of portrayal, Cocteau utilized the complete gamut of art forms: verse, drama, painting, music, novel, and, as his most preferred vehicle, cinema. Through the "discontinuous imagery" of his film-poetry, Cocteau sought to achieve what he termed the *Marvelous*—an atmosphere of magic and discovery proper for the audience assimilation of his poetic visions. And, once again, the death of the poet figures into Cocteau's artistry, for once the art work is given a life of its own, its creator can not survive in its presence without marring its effectiveness as a poetic medium. Thus, it is again through a series of figurative deaths that Cocteau achieved a concrete portrayal of his inspiration.

To further clarify Cocteau's complex artistic vocabulary, his relationship to his public was then investigated, as the final step of the poet's creative process. This notorious rapport between Cocteau and his antagonistic public gave birth to two of Cocteau's most fundamental pieces of poetic nomenclature: *invisibility* and *truthful lies*. The poet's "invisibility" stems from the dichotomized state of the poet's "public identity" versus his "true identity." According to Cocteau, not only the poet, but the poet's creations as well, oftentimes reflect this inherent "invisibility" as regards their respective public appreciation. Cocteau, thus, came to think of himself as a persecuted and quite misunderstood martyr, essentially altruistic yet invariably condemned for his efforts. It is perhaps as a result of these feelings on Cocteau's part that he came to refer to his craft as one of "truthful lies." The poet and his creations are but clever fabrications, ones that act as catalysts toward the attainment of higher truths. Such is the role of myth. And it is as a myth-creating, clownlike "lie which always tells the truth" that Cocteau tried to convey his poetry to a sceptical and unenlightened public, selecting the means by which he would most likely be able to succeed in his communicative endeavors.

Finally, drawing extensively from the preceding discussions, Cocteau's "Orphic identity" was examined. A composite "poetic" identity, an identity merging his own beliefs concerning the many deaths that a poet must endure to consummate his art, Cocteau came to define both himself and his art with his self-appointed mythic prototype of Orpheus. The many aspects of Cocteau's poetic philosophy, his technical theories, his "martyrdom" at the hands of his followers, and his very life-style seemed to provide sufficient motive for Cocteau to identify with the varying legends and heroic exploits of this Greek demigod. It was most probably via the writings of Rainer Maria Rilke that

Cocteau came into contact with the Orphic myth, and subsequently adapted it to himself and his works—the most notable of such cinematographic works being his highly autobiographical trilogy of film-poems entitled *Le Sang d'un Poète, Orphée,* and *Le Testament d'Orphée.*

It is these three film-poems, then, that were reinterpreted and re-evaluated as the concluding portion of this study. In contrast to the original American reception of these three cinematic works, a much more comprehensive and meaningful content was discovered therein, especially in the light of Cocteau's obviously autobiographical intent and his marked affiliation with the myth of Orpheus. *Le Sang d'un Poète, Orphée,* and *Le Testament d'Orphée,* thus, stand as a threefold cinematic legacy to the Orphic identity of their creator, and offer perhaps the clearest and most succinct portrait of Jean Cocteau-the-poet, as he had wished himself to be known for all time. Their story is his story, their composite identity is his identity, and their truths his truths. Viewed through the perspective of Orphic identity, one discovers within these three film-poems a lasting and quite revealing personal memorial to a now-legendary film-poet who, in terms of his innovative efforts within the art and poetry of the screen, must truly be considered one of the forefathers of the modern cinema of today, and that of tomorrow.

Bibliography

Books

Arnheim, Rudolph. *Film as Art*. Berkeley, California: University of California Press, 1966.

Bays, Gwendolyn. *The Orphic Vision*. Lincoln, Nebraska: University of Nebraska Press, 1964.

Bishop, John Peale. *The Collected Essays of John Peale Bishop*. Edited by Edmund Wilson. New York: Charles Scribner's Sons, 1948.

Bovay, G. M. *Cinéma; Un Oeil Ouvert sur le Monde*. Lausanne, Switz.: Editions Clairfontaine, 1952.

Brown, Frederick. *An Impersonation of Angels*. New York: Viking Press, 1968.

Campbell, Joseph. *Hero with a Thousand Faces*. Cleveland, Ohio: Meriden Press, 1964.

————. *The Masks of God; Occidental Mythology*. New York: Viking Press, 1964.

Cocteau, Jean. *Le Coq et l'Arlequin*. Paris: La Sirène, 1918.

————. *La Difficulté d'Etre*. Monaco: Editions du Rocher, 1957.

————. *The Difficulty of Being*. Translated by Elizabeth Sprigge. London: Peter Owens Publishers, 1966.

————. *Five Plays*. Translated by Carl Wildman, et al. New York: Hill and Wang, 1961.

————. *The Hand of a Stranger (Journal d'un Inconnu)*. Translated by Alec Brown. London: Elek Books, 1956.

————. *The Infernal Machine and Other Plays*. Translated by e. e. cummings, W. H. Auden, et al. New York: New Directions Books, 1963.

————. *The Journals of Jean Cocteau*. Edited and translated by Wallace Fowlie. Bloomington, Indiana: Indiana University Press, 1964.

————. *Lettre à Maritain*. Paris: Editions Stock, 1926.

————. *Opium: Journal of Intoxication*. Paris: Editions Stock, 1930.

————. *Orphée*. Paris: Editions André Bonne, 1951.

————. *Poésie*. Paris: Gallimard, 1925.

————. *Portraits-Souvenirs, 1900–1914*. Paris: Editions Grasset, 1935.

————. *Professional Secrets: An Autobiography of Jean Cocteau*. Edited by Robert Phelps. Translated by Richard Howard. New York: Farrar, Straus, and Giroux, 1970.

————. *Le Rappel à l'Ordre*. Paris: Editions Stock, 1926.

————. *Le Sang d'un Poète*. Monaco: Editions du Rocher, 1957.

————. *Le Testament d'Orphée*. Monaco: Editions du Rocher, 1961.

————. *Three Screenplays (L'Eternel Retour, Orphée, La Belle et La Bête)*. Translated by Carol Martin-Sperry. New York: Grossman Publishers, 1972.

————. *Two Screenplays: The Blood of a Poet, The Testament of Orpheus*. Translated by Carol Martin-Sperry. Baltimore, Maryland: Penguin Books, 1968.

Crosland, Margaret. *Jean Cocteau, A Biography*. London: Peter Nevill Editions, 1955.

Dodds, E. R. *The Greeks and the Irrational*. Boston: Beacon Press, 1951.

Dubourg, Pierre. *Dramaturgie de Jean Cocteau*. Paris: Bernard Grasset Editions, 1954.

Fergusson, Francis. *The Idea of a Theatre*. Princeton, New Jersey: Princeton University Press, 1949.

Fowlie, Wallace. *Age of Surrealism*. Bloomington, Indiana: Indiana University Press, 1966.

————. *Jean Cocteau: The History of a Poet's Age*. Bloomington, Indiana: Indiana University Press, 1961.

Fraigneau, André. *Cocteau*. Translated by Donald Lehmkuhl. New York: Grove Press, 1961.

————. *Cocteau on the Film*. Translated by Vera Traill. New York: Dover Publications, Inc., 1972.

————. *Cocteau par Lui-même*. Paris: Editions de Seuil, 1957.

————. *Entretiens Autour du Cinematographie*. Paris: Editions André Bonne, 1951.

Friedman, John Block. *Orpheus in the Middle Ages*. Cambridge, Massachusetts: Harvard University Press, 1970.

Geduld, Harry. *Filmmakers on Filmmaking*. Bloomington, Indiana: Indiana University Press, 1967.

Gilson, René. *Jean Cocteau*. Cinéma d'Aujourd'hui Series, no. 27. Translated by Ciba Vaughan. New York: Crown Publishers, Inc., 1964.

Grant, Michael. *Myths of the Greeks and Romans*. New York: Mentor Books, 1962.

Guthrie, W. K. C. *The Greeks and Their Gods*. Boston: Beacon Press, 1968.

Janin, J. B. *La Belle et la Bête, Journal d'un Film*. Monaco: Editions du Rocher, 1958.

Kael, Pauline. *Kiss Kiss Bang Bang*. Boston: Little, Brown, and Co., 1968.

Kaufmann, Stanley. *A World on Film*. New York: Harper and Row, 1966.

Kihm, Jean-Jacques. *Cocteau*. Paris: Editions Gallimard, 1960.

Knight, Arthur. *The Liveliest Art*. New York: Mentor Books, 1957.

Kushner, Eva. *Le Mythe d'Orphée dans la Littérature Française Contemporaine*. Paris: A. G. Nizet Publishers, 1961.

Langer, Susanne. *Feeling and Form*. New York: Charles Scribner's Sons, 1953.

Lannes, Roger. *Jean Cocteau*. Paris: Editions Seghers, 1968.

MacCann, Richard Dyer, ed. *Film: A Montage of Theories*. New York: E. P. Dutton and Co., 1966.

Manchel, Frank. *Film Study: A Resource Guide*. Cranbury, New Jersey: Fairleigh Dickinson University Press, 1973.

Mauriac, Claude. *Conversations with André Gide*. Translated by Michael Lebeck. New York: George Braziller Publishers, 1965.

————. *Jean Cocteau ou la Vérité du Mensonge*. Paris: Odette Lietier Publishers, 1945.

Millecam, Jean-Pierre. *L'Etoile de Jean Cocteau*. Monaco: Editions du Rocher, 1952.

Montagu, Ivor. *Film World*. Baltimore, Maryland: Penguin Books, 1968.

Mourgue, Gerard. *Jean Cocteau*. Paris: Editions Universitaires, 1965.

Oxenhandler, Neal. *Scandal and Parade: Theatre of Jean Cocteau*. New Brunswick, New Jersey: Rutgers University Press, 1957.

Pillaudin, Roger. *Jean Cocteau Tourne Son Dernier Film*. Paris: La Table Ronde, 1960.

Reinach, Salomon. *Orpheus: A History of Religions*. New York: Liveright Publishing Co., 1930.

Richardson, Robert. *Literature and Film*. Bloomington, Indiana: Indiana University Press, 1969.

Rilke, Rainer Maria. *Sonnets to Orpheus*. Translated by C. F. MacIntyre. Berkeley, California: University of California Press, 1967.

Sadoul, George. *Le Cinéma Français*. Paris: Editions Flammarion, 1962.

Sebeok, Thomas A. *Myth: A Symposium.* Bloomington, Indiana: Indiana University Press, 1958.

Sewell, Elizabeth. *The Orphic Voice.* New Haven, Connecticut: Yale University Press, 1960.

Sprigge, Elizabeth, and Kihm, Jean-Jacques. *Jean Cocteau: The Man and the Mirror.* New York: Coward-McCann, Inc., 1968.

Steegmuller, Francis. *Cocteau: A Biography.* Boston: Little, Brown, and Co., 1970.

Tyler, Parker. *Classics of the Foreign Film.* New York: Citadel Press, 1967.

————. *Magic and Myth of the Movies.* New York: Citadel Press, 1965.

Ward, Theodora. *Men and Angels.* New York: Viking Press, 1969.

Weisinger, Herbert. *The Agony and the Triumph: Papers on the Use and Abuse of Myth.* East Lansing, Michigan: Michigan State University Press, 1964.

Articles

Amberg, George. "The Testament of Cocteau." *Film Comment* 7, no. 4 (Winter 1971–72) : 23–27.

Beylie, Claude. "Jean Cocteau." In *Anthologie du Cinéma,* no. 12 (February 1968) , pp. 59–108.

Cesares, Maria. "On Cocteau as a Film Director." *World Theatre* 8 (Spring 1959) : 45–49.

Cocteau, Jean. "Le Menteur." In *Voix du Siècle.* Book 1. Edited by Eunice Clark Smith and John K. Savacool. New York: Harcourt, Brace, and World, 1960.

————. "Le Secret Professionnel." In *Le Rappel à l'Ordre.* Paris: Editions Stock, 1926.

Crowther, Bosley. "Orpheus." *New York Times,* 30 November 1950, p. 42.

————. "Testament of Orpheus." *New York Times,* 10 April 1962, p. 48.

Durgnat, Raymond. "Orphée." *Films and Filming* 10 (October 1963) : 45–49.

Hammond, Robert. "The Mysteries of Orpheus," *Cinema Journal* 11 (Spring 1972) : 26–33.

Kelman, Ken. "Film as Poetry." *Film Culture* 3, no. 29 (Summer 1963) : 22–27.

"Kubrick's Brilliant Vision." *Newsweek,* 3 January 1972, pp. 28–29.

Le Maitre, Henri. "Les Mythes Antiques en France." *Mosaic* 2/3 (Spring 1969) , pp. 25–41.

Maas, Willard. "Poetry and the Film: A Symposium." *Film Culture 3,* no. 27 (Winter 1962–63) : 55–63.

Manvell, Roger. "Le Testament d'Orphée." *Films and Filming 6* (July 1960) : 24.

Mekas, Jonas. "Hans Richter on the Nature of Film Poetry." *Film Culture 3,* no. 1 (Spring 1957) : 5–8.

Nin, Anais. "Poetics of the Film." *Film Culture 31* (Winter 1963–64) : 12–14.

Oxenhandler, Neal. "Jean Cocteau: Theatre as Parade." *Yale French Studies,* no. 14. New York: Drauss Corp., 1954–55.

————. "Poetry in Three Films of Cocteau." *Yale French Studies,* no. 17. New York: Drauss Corp., 1956.

Prouse, Derek. "Le Testament d'Orphée." *Sight and Sound 29* (Winter 1959–60) : 18–19.

Smith, Harry T. "A Cocteau Concoction." *New York Times,* 3 November 1933, p. 23.

"Le Testament d'Orphée." *Fiche Filmographique.* Institut des Hautes Etudes Cinématographiques, Paris, 1961.

Wallis, C. G. "The Blood of a Poet." *Kenyon Review 6,* no. 1 (Winter 1944) : 25–42.

Miscellaneous

Letter to Arthur Evans by Claude Pinoteau, technical director of Jean Cocteau's *Le Testament d'Orphée,* 6 August 1971.

Petit Larousse. Paris: Librarie Larousse, 1967.

Photostat of original manuscript of *Le Testament d'Orphée,* used with the permission of Dr. Robert Hammond, curator of the Hammond Film Script Collection housed in the Memorial Library of the State University of New York at Cortland.

Taped interview with Dr. Neal Oxenhandler of Dartmouth College, 2 August 1971.

Text of speech given by Dr. Robert Hammond, State University of New York, at The Society of Cinema Studies annual convention held in Montreal, Canada, during March 1971.

Webster's New Collegiate Dictionary. 2nd edition. Springfield, Massachusetts: G. and C. Merriam Co., 1956.

Index

Acrobats, 54, 137; as metaphor for poet's discipline, 42; poet as intermediary, 148. *See also* Barbette; Angels-Angelism

Age d'Or, L' by Luis Bunuel, 46, 87

Aglaonice: in *Orphée* (play), 66; in *Orphée* (film), 116–17, 120, 122

Ange Heurtebise, L': and death of Radiquet, 99; as source of metaphor "angel," 80–81

Angels-Angelism, 28, 37–38, 41–42, 72, 137, 143, 148, 163; and Orpheus myth, 76; characteristics of, 34–35; origins for Cocteau, 39, 80–81; in *Orphée*, 119, 122, 126; poet's inspiration and, 33, 36, 39–40, 52; in *Sang d'un Poète*, 96–97, 99; studies done on, 35n. *See also* Acrobats; Beyond; Inspiration

Antigone, 37, 49, 65

Apollinaire, Guillaume, 42, 91

Apollo: cult of Orphism and, 71; *Orphée*, 109; Orpheus as worshipper of, 68–69, 70, 75, 82

Argonautica, by Appollonius, 67

Argonauts, Orpheus and, 68, 70, 109

Bacchus, 43, 65

Bal du Comte d'Orgel, Le, by Raymond Radiquet, 37

Barbette, 42, 64

Belle et la Bête, La (Beauty and the Beast), 41, 43, 50, 106

Bérard, Christian, 41

Bernhardt, Sarah, 150–51

Beyond, the, 34–35, 39, 42, 49, 72, 74, 163; and definition of poetry, 31–32, 163; poet as vehicle for, 32–34, 148, 163; poet's "night," 32–33, 40, 76, 130, 142, 161, 163. *See also* Angels-Angelism; Inspiration; Portrayal; Public

Blood, 44, 94–96, 137, 157; in *Sang d'un Poète*, 94

Cégeste: in *Orphée*, 102, 109, 111, 113, 116, 120; in *Le Testament d'Orphée*, 135–40, 142–45, 150–60

Cendrars, Blaise, 80

Chanel, CoCo, 151

Chevaliers de la Table Ronde, Les, 33, 43

Chien Andalou, Un, 20, 22–23

Christ: as metaphor for poet, 39, 54, 74, 80, 105, 137, 148, 158–59, 161; and *Orphée* (play), 104–5; and Orphic Identity, 105, 113, 161. *See also* Orphic Identity; Public

Clockwork Orange, A, 18

Cocteau, Jean: acrobats, 42; and his "angel," 33–35; biography of, 30, 30n; as "bricoleur," 81; cinematic technique, 47–49; as film-maker, 27, 145–53; as forefather of modern cinema, 26–28, 168; influence of the theater, 63–64; invisibility, 56–59; making of *Orphée*, 102–9; making of *Sang d'un Poète*, 45–47, 84–89; making of *Testament d'Orphée*, 129–32; Marvelous, 42–43; misogyny, 113; and opium, 36–37; and Radiquet, 37–39; relation to public, 53–65; relationship with Orpheus, 65–83; religion and Jacques Maritain, 39, 54; and Rainer Maria Rilke, 79–82; sense of artistic discipline, 40–41; studies done as a literary figure, 27–28; and Surrealists,

171